PYTHONS AND BOAS

PETER J. STAFFORD

The author feels strongly that, in the case of wild-caught specimens, pythons and boas should be kept only as part of planned captive breeding programs. Due to the destruction of habitat and over-collecting for the skin trade they are becoming too rare in nature to be kept merely as interesting pets. Their very size and often irascible temperament also argue against them being handled by inexperienced persons. Pictures of models with large snakes in this book were taken under the supervision of experienced handlers and do not represent the way in which most large snakes should be handled.

Title page: Close-up of the common boa constrictor, *Boa constrictor constrictor*. Photo by P. J. Stafford.

© 1986 by T.F.H. Publications, Inc. Ltd.

Distributed in the UNITED STATES by T.F.H. Publications, Inc., 211 West Sylvania Avenue, Neptune City, NJ 07753; in CANADA by H & L Pet Supplies Inc., 27 Kingston Crescent, Kitchener, Ontario N2B 2T6; Rolf C. Hagen Ltd., 3225 Sartelon Street, Montreal 382 Quebec; in ENGLAND by T.F.H. Publications Limited, 4 Kier Park, Ascot, Berkshire SL5 7DS; in AUSTRALIA AND THE SOUTH PACIFIC by T.F.H. (Australia) Pty. Ltd., Box 149, Brookvale 2100 N.S.W., Australia; in NEW ZEALAND by Ross Haines & Son, Ltd., 18 Monmouth Street, Grey Lynn, Auckland 2 New Zealand; in SINGAPORE AND MALAYSIA by MPH Distributors (S) Pte., Ltd., 601 Sims Drive, # 03/07/21, Singapore 1438; in the PHILIPPINES by Bio-Research, 5 Lippay Street, San Lorenzo Village, Makati Rizal; in SOUTH AFRICA by Multipet Pty. Ltd., 30 Turners Avenue, Durban 4001. Published by T.F.H. Publications Inc. Manufactured in the United States of America by T.F.H. Publications, Inc.

Contents

Foreword

I wonder how many visitors to the zoo have paused in the reptile house to marvel at a large python or boa neatly coiled in deceitful slumber behind the glass partition. Suffice to say that quite possibly no other group of animals inspires such an overwhelming curiosity bordering on revulsion than do those commonly referred to as the "giant snakes." It is the intention of this book not only to provide an insight into the fascinating world of these creatures, but also to encourage the growing interest in keeping reptiles principally for captive breeding purposes rather than just simply as pets or exhibits.

Pythons and boas represent just a small percentage of the snakes alive today, forming a diversified group that has adapted to contend with all manner and combination of life-styles; some are ground-dwellers or semi-aquatic in habits, while others live in the trees or under the soil. They comprise a large number of small and unusual varieties in addition to the impressive giants that always attract so much attention.

The book has been divided into three main topics discussing the lives of pythons and boas, the snakes themselves, and lastly how they are cared for in captivity. It is appreciated that some readers actively concerned with wildlife conservation may question the morality of keeping snakes, as they would any other wild animal, in confinement, but to this end I hope the following pages will go some way to proclaim the value and importance of captive breeding, especially in view of the serious survival threats faced now by a great many species the world over.

Facing page: The pythons and boas are undoubtedly the most popular pet reptiles, but with increasing demands there must come a new responsibility on the part of the owners and retailers to have the animals breed in captivity. Photo by J. Dodd of *Eunectes murinus.*

Acknowledgments

For their invaluable help and cooperation in preparing this book, the author is particularly indebted to the following: Dr. E. N. Arnold, A. F. Stimson, and Dr. C. J. McCarthy (Reptile Section, British Museum of Natural History); R. A. Ford (International Trade in Endangered Species Branch, Department of the Environment, U.K.); Anthony Grahame; Dr. H. G. Cogger (Deputy Director, Australian Museum); Phillip Coffey (Jersey Wildlife Preservation Trust); Dr. W. R. Branch (Department of Herpetology, Port Elizabeth Museum, South Africa); R. T. Hoser; and J. P. Swaak.

Grateful thanks are also due to the publishers for their courtesy and help in preparing the manuscript, the reptile keepers at Chester Zoo, and to those friends and other zoological institutions who allowed me to photograph their animals.

I would also like to thank the various members of my family for their help and encouragement, especially my mother, Wyn, for typing much of the final draft, my father, Peter, and my brother, David, all of whom contributed greatly in bringing the project to fruition.

Facing page: Of the more than 80 species of pythons and boas, only a dozen or so are regularly available to hobbyists, one of the more common being *Epicrates cenchria maurus* from northwestern South America. Photo by J. Dodd.

1: Natural History

INTRODUCTION

Pythons and boas, known scientifically as the family Boidae, seem to have originated at least by the Upper Cretaceous Period. They are a successful but primitive group of snakes that almost certainly derive, oddly enough, from lizards with long and well-developed limbs. These lizards branched off during the late Mesozoic to pursue a new and different life-style beneath the forest floor. As their habits and behavior became progressively oriented toward an existence below the ground, so too did the physical structure of the body change. The number of vertebrae in particular increased (although it may still be fewer than some lizards) and the limbs, by now more of a handicap than of practical use in burrowing, receded in favor of a streamlined shape to facilitate ease of movement through the soil. Adaptive modifications of cranial structures and the teeth also occurred, accompanied by regression in the senses of sight and hearing, which hold little value to life in such a dark and silent world. For reasons not yet fully explained, this transformation was followed by a gradual return to life above the surface, ultimately giving rise to the broad cross-section of snakes with which we are all to some extent familiar.

To substantiate this sequence of events, boids can be linked with their long-extinct predecessors through the rare and unique Bornean earless monitor (*Lanthanotus*

They may not look very snake-like, but the monitors (above, *Lanthanotus borneensis,* photo by J. T. Collins; below, *Varanus komodoensis,* photo by Dr. S. A. Minton) are closely related to the ancestors of the boas and other snakes.

borneensis). While the affinities of this lizard with others of its kind (especially the varanids or monitors) are clearly evident, *Lanthanotus* also shares a significant number of features with snakes and appears to be the nearest surviving relative of the common ancestor from which it is believed all snakes evolved.

Ancestral forms of pythons, boas, and their extinct relatives are well represented in the fossilized deposits of the Upper Cretaceous and succeeding eras. Some are known to have measured in the region of 50 to 100 feet and must have been formidable creatures. Modern descendants are very much smaller but have otherwise changed little in 70 million years.

Boids are one of the few ophidian families that possess rudimentary vestiges of the pelvic girdle and hind limbs, a lingering relic of their past history. The greatly reduced hind limbs are visible as small claw-like processes called pelvic spurs on either side of the cloacal opening. Those of the male are often larger and may play an important role in the events leading up to copulation.

The flexible backbone is comprised of approximately 200 to over 400 vertebrae, each connected to the next by no less than five individual joints. The vertebral segments are all very similar, and apart from the first few behind the head and those of the tail, each supports a pair of ribs.

The internal organs are similar to those of other vertebrates but are elongated and arranged in a somewhat displaced manner to suit the narrow serpentine form. The stomach in particular is tube-like in appearance and capable of great distension. Larger species of pythons and boas possess two functional lungs. In boas the left lung is generally reduced, but some pythons are bestowed with two of almost equal capacity. Males possess a paired genital organ that is split to the base, only one

Above: *Python spilotes*, the carpet python, a fairly typical representative of the family Boidae. Photo by Dr. S. A. Minton, **Below:** The pelvic spurs of *Epicrates striatus*, leg remnants found in virtually all boids. Photo by J. Dodd.

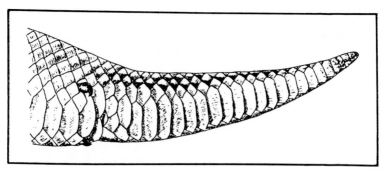

The pelvic spurs are found in both sexes of pythons and boas (with the Round Island boas and females of some *Tropidophis* about the only exceptions) but are usually larger in males. They are believed to be used as copulatory stimulants during mating behavior. Art by P. J. Stafford.

division of which is engaged during mating. The halves of this paired structure, known as hemipenes, are often equipped with frills and spines to ensure firm anchorage in the female's cloaca. They can be used to help distinguish particular species because they show much variation between different species but are usually very constant in a single species.

The family Boidae contains what are probably the most familiar and certainly the largest of all living snakes. Geographically they are virtually confined to tropical or subtropical climates because only high and fairly constant temperatures can sustain such relatively large reptiles. They are a diversified group occurring in a wide variety of habitats ranging from the arid deserts of Australia to the humid rainforests of South America. Some species have even adapted to life around human habitations, subsisting on vermin and domestic fowl.

Although the family encompasses many small and unusual species, it is renowned for those giant serpents

Facing page: The green or common anaconda, *Eunectes murinus,* seldom exceeds 20 feet in length, but a few rare giants over 30 feet long have been reliably reported. Although reticulated pythons may equal or slightly exceed this length, the anaconda is much the heavier of the two species and is undoubtedly the largest (as opposed to longest) living snake. Top photo by Dr. M. Freiberg; bottom photo by J. Dodd.

whose awesome size has captivated the imagination of romantic novelists throughout history. Most early travelers' tales of monsters reaching lengths of up to 100 feet, however, are today regarded with justifiable skepticism, for the largest examples of living boids have been authentically recorded to have measured well under 40 feet long. There are two species that compete for the title of "largest snake," the reticulated python *(Python reticulatus)* and the anaconda *(Eunectes murinus)*. The former is believed by most scientists to grow a little longer, but the anaconda attains a far greater weight. There are very few species of boids that pose a realistic threat to human life, although this does not deny the fact that fatal encounters, infrequent though they may be, do occur. Not unnaturally, incidents of attacks on humans have been the subject of much conjecture and exaggeration, but there is certainly truth in the allegations that large boids may sometimes be responsible for the mysterious disappearance of people in Africa, Asia, and South America. Confirmed reports usually involve young children, as specimens capable of overpowering a healthy adult are extremely rare indeed. Accidental deaths also occur on occasion due to mishandling of large boids in captivity.

Pythons and boas often play a major role in the religious activities of tribal peoples. They are also eaten by many people, particularly in Oriental countries where they are regarded as something of a delicacy. The most serious form of exploitation, however, is the highly organized and often illegal international trade in tanned snake skins. Populations of the larger species have suffered considerably for decades and still constitute a sizable portion of the skin market. The number of skins marketed illegally in past years may have run into many hundreds of thousands, but fortunately the situation has gradually started to improve with the advent of CITES

A juvenile reticulated python, *Python reticulatus*, showing the character-istic narrow median line on the head. Photo by P. J. Stafford.

17

legislation and subsequent introduction of new regulations that are being enforced both in the countries where the skins originate and where they are ultimately sold as luxury consumer items such as shoes and handbags.

The Boidae is usually divided into seven subfamilies: Pythoninae (pythons); Boinae (large boas); Calabariinae (burrowing python); Erycinae (sand, rosy, and rubber boas); Loxoceminae (Mexican python); Tropidophiinae (wood snakes and dwarf boas); and Bolyeriinae (Round Island boas). Some herpetologists would recognize the last three subfamilies as full families, but for the sake of argument we will stick with a conservative approach. For the benefit of newcomers to the science of herpetology, those species that are most likely to be met with in a practical context will be found in the first four subfamilies mentioned, and these have consequently received greater attention.

While not entirely diagnostic, the most obvious characteristic that distinguishes pythons from boas lies in their method of reproduction. All pythons are oviparous, producing leathery-shelled eggs in an early stage of embryonic development. Once the eggs have been laid, the female python gathers them into a heap and encircles the mound with her coils, finally bringing her head to rest on top. After a few hours the eggs stick together, an adaptation that reduces the exposed surface area and inhibits the evaporation of water vital for successful development. The females of several species not only protect their clutches of eggs but actually "incubate" them, a phenomenon associated with no other reptile. This is achieved by spasmodic "twitching" of

Overleaf: *Python curtus brongersmai.* Photo by P. J. Stafford.
Facing page: *Python regius,* the royal or ball python, is a relatively small species that is sometimes very common on the pet market and does well in captivity. Photo by J. Dodd.

the muscles in the coiled snake that increases the temperature in the immediate vicinity of the eggs by as much as 12° F. The young python breaks out of the egg with the aid of an egg tooth, a small, sharp projection on the snout that cuts through the shell and is cast off soon after hatching.

Python oviparity is not an ideal reproductive process and is generally considered to be evolutionarily inferior to that of boas, whose young are born fully developed and lead an independent life from the very start. Female pythons of most species are compelled to remain coiled about their eggs until such time as they hatch and are consequently in greater potential danger than are female boas, which have no maternal obligations. Furthermore, newly born boas are able to disperse within minutes of birth, while the young python must survive the final stages of development incarcerated in an egg from which it cannot escape until ready to hatch.

Pythons are further separated from boas by the presence of a small bone above the eye known as the supra-orbital bone. Unlike boas, most larger pythons lack teeth on the premaxillae, a pair of bones located in the anteriormost portion of the upper jaw. As a rule, the upper surface of the head in pythons is covered with large symmetrical plates rather than the bead-like scales typical of most boas, but this is really quite variable. Pythons generally possess paired rows of subcaudal scales compared to a single column in boas.

These snakes have evolved into one of the most sophisticated groups of all predatory animals. The reason for their success and why they have held their own against more advanced snakes can be attributed to a number of morphological adaptations that assist in the detection and location of prey. Perhaps the most extraordinary adaptation, although one not found in all boids, is a series of heat-sensitive depressions in the la-

One of the most fascinating but frustrating of the boids is the emerald or green tree boa, *Corallus caninus*. First, the species is an almost exact South American analog of the not closely related New Guinea green tree python, *Chondropython*. The similarity between the two extends to coloration, general proportions, very unusual method of coiling about a branch, and even the presence of differently colored young. In captivity the species often is excessively aggressive and may be difficult to feed, but it has now been bred in a few zoos. In this photo the heat-sensing labial pits are very prominent and readily seen; few other boids have these pits so obviously visible.

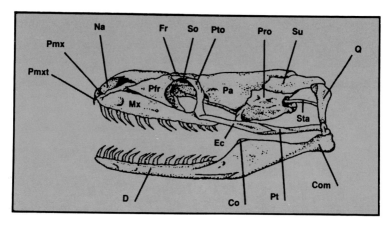

The skull of the reticulated python, *Python reticulatus* (modified from Bellairs). Co – coronoid; Com – compound; D – dentary; Ec – ectopterygoid; Fr – frontal; Mx – maxilla; Na – nasal; Pa – parietal; Pfr – prefrontal; Pmx – premaxilla; Pmxt – premaxillary teeth; Pro – prootic; Pt – pterygoid; Pto – Postorbital; Q – quadrate; So – supraorbital or postfrontal; Su – squamosal or temporal; Sta – stapes.

bial scales of the upper and lower jaws. These organs are highly sensitive to infrared wavelengths and can detect the slightest change in temperature. Each pit is directed at a different angle to provide the widest possible field of reception and collectively are of unequaled assistance at night in pinpointing the exact position of warm-blooded prey, although only at fairly close range. This means of locating food has also arisen in the venomous pit vipers, including the rattlesnakes.

All snakes have an acute sense of smell for which they are indebted to Jacobson's organ. This organ, a paired olfactory structure situated in the roof of the mouth, is concerned with the analysis of chemical samples taken at regular intervals from the atmosphere. The tongue, one of whose functions is to collect and deliver these samples, also acts as a device for touch.

Snakes are incapable of producing modulated sounds. Although they lack external ear openings and are largely deaf to airborne sound, they can nonetheless hear in the broad sense of the word, differing from higher verte-

Two ground boas typical of dry habitats. **Above:** *Lichanura trivirgata.*
Photo by R. Haas. **Below:** *Eryx conicus.* Photo by J. Dodd.

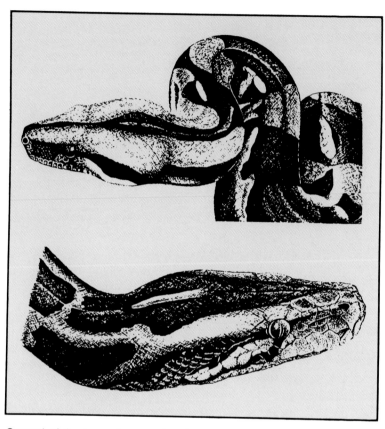

Several of the larger boas and pythons possess basically similar color patterns, especially on the head. Shown at top is *Boa constrictor;* at bottom is *Python molurus bivittatus.* Art by P. J. Stafford.

brates only in the route by which sound is transmitted. The quadrate and lower jaw bones, comparable with the mammalian eardrum, act as a mechanism for channeling ground vibration through the stapes bone to the inner ear.

Facing page: Although many boids are found in relatively dry areas, the larger species are characteristically found near water. Tropical rivers and floodplains, whether in the Brazilian Amazon (top, photo by Dr. H. R. Axelrod) or the forests of Thailand (bottom, photo by Dr. R. Geisler) are likely to be the home of at least one larger boid, whether an anaconda, boa constrictor, or python.

Overall, vision in snakes is quite well-developed but the eyes do not seem to perceive stationary objects and will only register movement at fairly close range. Pythons and boas possess vertically slit pupils, an adaptation to a nocturnal way of life. Diurnal snakes rely much more heavily on visual detection of prey and usually have round pupils. Snakes lack true eyelids, which have been replaced by a single transparent scale, the brille, that completely encloses the eye.

FEEDING

Boid snakes are opportunistic feeders, preferring by choice to lie in wait for their prey rather than seek it out. Prey is dispatched by means of constriction: the victim is seized in the jaws by an almost imperceptibly fast strike and is quickly enveloped by the muscular coils, which then tighten to prevent the ribs, diaphragm, lungs, and heart from functioning. Asphyxiation follows rapidly.

Snakes, especially the larger boids, are able to consume exceptionally large animals in their entirety. The cranial bones are flexible and loosely hinged to absorb pressure incurred when swallowing, and the lower jaws are able to dislocate from the skull, making it a fairly easy matter to engulf prey much larger than would be normally thought possible. The bones of the lower jaw in particular do not culminate in a solid chin as with most other vertebrates, but are more or less free, allowing both vertical and horizontal movement. Snakes begin eating at the head, gradually "walking" over their prey by alternate forward-stretching movements of the upper and lower jaws, assisted by a copious flow of saliva. Food is drawn into the throat with the aid of sharp, recurved teeth and then manipulated into the digestive tract by muscular undulations against the esophageal wall. It is not uncommon for teeth to break off during

The majority of boids feed on small mammals and birds both in nature and in captivity. **Above:** *Epicrates striatus;* photo by J. T. Kellnhauser. **Below:** Juvenile *Epicrates cenchria crassus;* photo by Dr. M. Freiberg.

the capture and subjugation of prey. Fixed rigidly to the jaw, they are subject to a great deal of wear but as a matter of course are replaced naturally if lost or damaged. The scale-clad skin of snakes is tremendously elastic by nature and does not hinder swallowing in the slightest. Complete digestion of food takes on average from four to six days, depending on the prevailing temperature and the size of the meal.

Pythons and boas can survive without food for considerable periods of time. Indeed, it is not unusual for captive specimens to refuse food for several weeks or even months yet lose only a fraction of their body weight. Some exceptional individuals are known to have fasted for more than a year without any apparent ill effects. In equatorial regions where seasonal heat is severe, fasting may occur naturally at fixed cyclic intervals. Just as reptiles of the Northern Hemisphere hibernate during colder months, many tropical reptiles estivate underground or in a hollow tree to escape the heat of mid-summer. This is especially true of anacondas (*Eunectes* sp.), which burrow into the wet mud of river banks during periods of drought to emerge again only when the rains return. Sand boas (*Eryx* sp.) have also been known to estivate, burrowing deeply into loose sand or hiding away in rodent burrows and beneath rocks. Even captive boids kept at uniform temperatures throughout the year may lose their appetite and become withdrawn in preparation for a period of dormancy, although it may never be actually undertaken.

LONGEVITY

Evidence from records kept for captive specimens seems to suggest that pythons and boas are perhaps the longest-lived of all snakes. Some individuals are known to have lived for almost 30 years, although the average

Given the proper care, hatchling boas and pythons can undoubtedly mature in captivity to produce healthy adults that can be bred to relieve the pressure on natural populations. Remember that children should never be allowed to handle large snakes without proper supervision. Photo of *Boa constrictor constrictor* by K. Freeman.

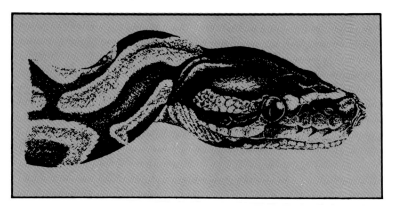

Head study of the characteristic facial pattern of *Python regius*. Art by P. J. Stafford.

age for the larger species is nearer to 20. Unlike birds and mammals, growth may never completely cease even after sexual maturity has been reached, but overall size can not be taken as an accurate indication of age because the rate of growth is dependent upon health, temperature, and intake of food, among other factors.

MOVEMENT

Of all the "mysterious" qualities surrounding the sinister character of snakes, it is their method of moving more than any other trait that inspires the deep revulsion felt by many people toward these animals. There is however, nothing "supernatural" about the way in which they move, albeit without the aid of limbs. Indeed, the basic mechanics of locomotion are in fact quite simple and easy to comprehend.

Boids employ three methods of locomotion. Heavy-bodied terrestrial varieties use what is termed a rectilinear technique, *i.e.*, creeping forward in a straight line. The powerful muscles between the ribs and ventral scales contract backward from the neck in a rippling motion, pushing the snake forward. The second technique involves using the rear third of the body to push the anterior portion forward. The tail-end is then drawn

A juvenile Cook's tree boa, *Corallus enydris cookii,* from a captive breeding. Photo by P. J. Stafford.

up to the advanced position and the movement is repeated. Finally, the typical serpentine method as used by most other snakes is chiefly employed when swimming and can best be described as a continuous "S" movement. On land the apex of each loop is used to push against irregularities of the terrain. This method is more advanced and superior to the others described and has been mastered by the higher families of snakes. Some members of the Colubridae, the largest snake family, can move surprisingly quickly even over relatively smooth surfaces.

COLORATION

Pythons and boas exhibit none of the garish colors displayed, for example, by certain birds, lizards, and butterflies. They cannot move quickly and need to hide as best they can among the leaves on the forest floor or in the trees so as to stay hidden from enemies and retain the element of surprise should some unsuspecting prey chance to wander by. Coloration is therefore restricted in most cases to somber shades of red, brown, green, and yellow, usually marbled with blotches, spots, and stripes to disrupt the outline of the snake. Interestingly enough, males and females do not differ in color, although many individual species show a wide range of colors. A prime example is the garden tree boa (*Corallus enydris*) from South America that varies from orange-brown through uniform shades of gray to almost black. To a certain degree, boids are able to voluntarily lighten or darken their appearance according to mood and environmental factors but remain incapable of changing specific colors in the "chameleon fashion" typical of many lizards. Some species bear a striking resemblance in pattern to poisonous snakes. Whether this is a deliberate attempt to increase their chances of survival or simply coincidental is a little unclear, but legitimate or other-

A juvenile rough-scaled Pacific island boa, *Candoia carinata*. The pattern in this juvenile is much more sharply defined than in the adult. Photo by J. Gee.

wise it certainly does not compare with the mimicry achieved by, for example, the tricolored kingsnakes *(Lampropeltis)* that imitate the highly venomous coral snakes *(Micrurus* and *Micruroides)* so deceptively. To give but two examples of possible mimicry among boids, the rough-scaled sand boa *(Eryx conicus)* has a viper-like zig-zag stripe down the back, and the garden tree boa *(Corallus e. enydris)* has been likened to the deadly fer-de-lance *(Bothrops atrox)* found in the same localities.

Certain boids produce offspring whose coloration is entirely different from that of their parents. This phenomenon is perhaps best illustrated by the green tree python *(Chondropython viridis)*, whose young are yellow or brownish at birth and do not develop the characteristic green coloration of adults until at least two years of age.

SHEDDING

The epidermal layer of the reptilian skin is comprised largely of keratin, a dead and virtually inflexible material that needs to be shed every so often to enable continuous growth. Shedding or sloughing, as this process is called, takes place regularly among fast-growing juveniles but occurs less frequently as they near maturity. Snakes approaching a shed secrete a lubricant that collects under the outer layer of skin, producing a cloudy effect most obviously noticeable over the eye (which may appear quite blue). During this vulnerable time the snake will often retire and stop feeding for several days until vision has been fully restored, shortly after which shedding will commence. Abrasive objects such as rocks and pieces of bark are used to help split the skin over the snout, and as the snake moves around the old skin layer gradually peels back over the length of the body, turning itself inside out.

Boids are not noted for their spectacular colors. Very few species are as brightly colored as the rainbow boa (above, *Epicrates cenchria cenchria*), but admittedly few are as plain as the Australian water python (*Liasis mackloti "fuscus"*) shown below. Photo above by G. Marcuse; that below by Dr. S. A. Minton.

Captive snakes that experience difficulty in shedding should be sprayed or restrained in a bath of warm water to help loosen the skin, which can then be carefully removed manually. A freshly shed snake is usually exceptionally brilliant and colorful.

GENERAL HABITS AND ENEMIES

Pythons and boas are for the most part solitary animals that only associate during the mating season to copulate. They are mainly nocturnal and crepuscular in habits, though some may forsake their sanctuary to bask if the weather turns unfavorably cool. In common with all reptiles and amphibians, the level of heat generated by their own body's metabolism falls well short of that required to sustain active life and needs to be compensated by other means. Reptiles of cooler temperate latitudes must seek to regulate their body temperature through basking in the sun and absorbing heat liberated by the environment. In tropical climates the optimum temperature, *i.e.*, that at which the body operates most effectively, is easier to maintain by virtue of the fact that ambient temperatures remain fairly constant throughout the year and do not fall too sharply at night.

In point of fact, tropical species are more often faced with the problem of how to reduce their body heat rather than how to increase it. The consequences of over-heating in reptiles are far more serious than those arising from excessive cold. A victim weakened by heat exhaustion will soon die if unable to find refuge from the intense heat of midday in the tropics.

Contrary to popular opinion, pythons and boas seldom defend themselves by coiling around and attempting to constrict a would-be aggressor, preferring to discourage an enemy by inflating the body, striking savagely, and generally acting in an intimidating manner. Some species are able to secrete an odious musk

Australian pythons tend to be found near water like most other pythons, but because of the tendency of many Australian rivers to become virtually dry during part of the year (above) they must be more adaptable than species living in more stable environments. Photos by Dr. G. R. Allen.

from anal glands as a further deterrent. The most usual method of defense, however, is to simply avoid detection by withdrawing from sight as discretely as possible or remaining perfectly motionless and relying on camouflage.

Boid snakes are to a certain extent territorial. It is not unusual for arboreal species in particular to settle in the neighborhood of a favorite roosting site for several months or even years. Similarly, terrestrial species will usually stay in one area for as long as environmental conditions remain suitable and the supply of food endures.

Small species of boids and the young of larger varieties fall prey to a mixed selection of predators, including hawks, other snakes, crocodilians, mongooses, storks, and pigs. Domesticated pigs in particular are capable of inflicting serious damage to established habitats if allowed to forage for food unchecked. Since their introduction to Round Island in the Indian Ocean, wild populations of the two endemic boas *Casarea dussumieri* and *Bolyeria multocarinata* have declined virtually beyond recovery in a very short space of time, having been both killed in great numbers and deprived of suitable habitat. Fortunately, their plight has now been recognized and steps are being taken to establish breeding colonies in captivity.

DISTRIBUTION AND LIFE-STYLE

While there are a few areas where pythons and boas occur together, it is of considerable evolutionary significance that the two groups occupy relatively clear-cut and almost exclusive geographical ranges. As a rule, pythons predominate in the "Old World," but boas are associated more with the Americas of the "New World." Only in the Indonesian islands and New Guinea area do the true boas and pythons (Boinae and Pythoninae) co-

Distribution of the true boas, subfamily Boinae.

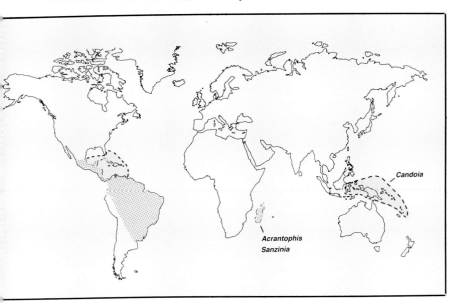

Distribution of the ground boas, subfamily Erycinae.

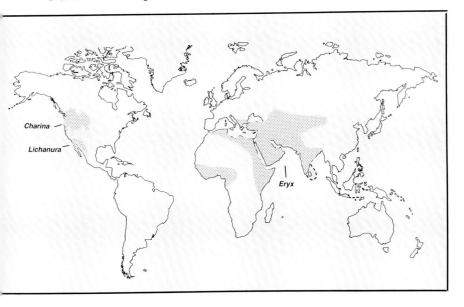

exist, and even here they tend to occupy different habitats. Sand boas (Erycinae) co-occur with pythons, Boinae occurs on Madagascar sandwiched between areas generally inhabited by pythons, and Boinae and Loxoceminae as well as Tropidophiinae are sympatric.

Terrestrial and semiarboreal life-styles embrace by far the majority of species, but nonetheless a good many have progressed to a life almost exclusively in the trees, water, or underground to exploit different sources of food. Ground-dwelling snakes tend to be heavily built and extremely well camouflaged to avoid discovery while at rest or awaiting prey. It would also be true to say that many of the larger varieties are to some extent semiaquatic. Snakes are attracted to water principally as a means of obtaining food, for some degree of protection, and for help in stabilizing their body temperature, but large individuals may also secure physical support from the water's buoyancy. Indeed, it is quite possible that this may in part explain why some water-loving boids are able to grow to such tremendous sizes. The anacondas (genus *Eunectes*) from South America are the only boids that can be defined as predominantly aquatic in habits. Unlike "aquatically oriented" terrestrial species such as many of the large pythons, the eyes and nostrils of anacondas are positioned somewhat higher on the head for ease of seeing and breathing when the rest of the body is all but submerged.

There are comparatively few species that are adapted to a specialized existence high up in the trees. Genuine tree-dwelling boids are characterized by a slender, laterally compressed body and a strongly prehensile tail for ease of movement through the branches. The eyes are large and the head well-defined from the neck. Almost without exception, arboreal boids prey heavily upon birds and have developed greatly enlarged front teeth to penetrate a thick coat of feathers and be sure of a firm

Distribution of the burrowing pythons, subfamilies Calabariinae and Loxoceminae.

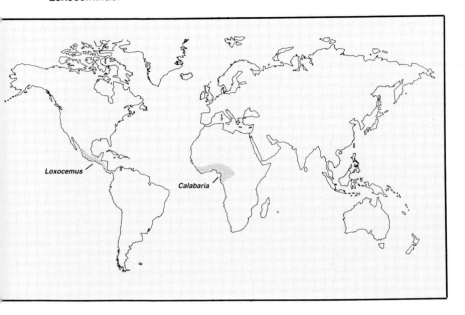

Distribution of the true pythons, subfamily Pythoninae.

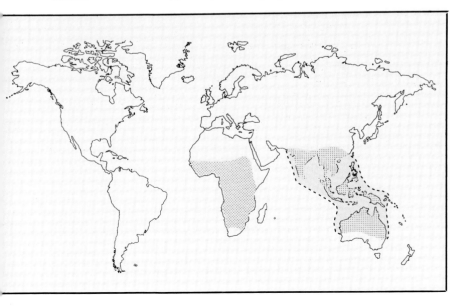

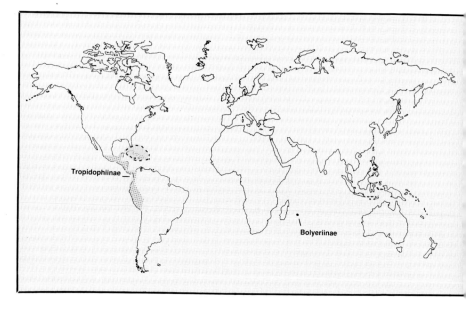

Distribution of dwarf boas, subfamilies Tropidophiinae and Bolyeriinae.

hold. Camouflage again plays an important part in their survival by concealing them from enemies and providing disguise until prey is close enough to be seized. The majority of tree-dwelling species inhabit the dense understory of smaller shrubs and bushes, where food is generally more abundant and escape from predators easier, in preference to the forest canopy.

Having progressed from an ancestral existence beneath the ground, some species have reverted to a semi-fossorial (burrowing) life in pursuit of new sources of food, while still taking advantage of behaviors and adaptations developed above the surface. Typical burrowing species can perhaps best be described as small, stout forms with a cylindrical body, blunt tail, and inconspicuous head. The eyes are normally reduced and the snout bluntly pointed or wedge-shaped, often with a hardened rostral scale to assist in burrowing. Furthermore, the nostrils of some are positioned in such a way as to pre-

In tropical countries the large above-ground nests of termites are the favored habitats for numerous animals of all shapes and sizes, including some species of boids that either feed here or retreat here during the heat of the day. Photo by Dr. G. R. Allen.

vent fine sand or particles of soil from obstructing the breathing passages. Burrowing snakes are to be found mainly in areas of loose, dry subsoil or in rodent and termite galleries, but some, such as the sand boas (genus *Eryx*), have undergone further modifications that enable them to survive in the desert.

2:Pythoninae— True Pythons

GENUS *PYTHON*

Most of the really large snakes, by which is meant those that exceed 10 feet in length, rank among a group known as the "true pythons," of which the largest group is the genus *Python*, numbering 13 species distributed over much of the greater part of Africa, India, Southeast Asia, and Australia. Excluding the reticulated python *(Python reticulatus)*, the African and Asian forms are rather stout in relation to length and lead a predominantly terrestrial life. The Indo-Australian species, on the other hand, tend to be more slender in build and somewhat more arboreal in habits. Pythons of this genus are generally cylindrical in cross-section. The tail is strongly prehensile, and the subcaudal scales are mainly divided.

Of the three species to be found in Africa, the **African rock python** *(Python sebae)* is by far the largest, reaching between 10 and almost 20 feet in length. The dorsal surface is patterned with various shades of brown complemented by an irregular series of bolder stripes and blotches. The head coloration is characterized by a dark arrowhead-like blotch on the top bordered on ei-

Facing page: **Top:** *Python sebae sebae,* the African rock python. Photo by J. K. Langhammer. **Bottom:** *Python sebae natalensis,* the rock python of southern Africa. Photo by Dr. W. R. Branch.

ther side by a pale stripe. The ventral surface is whitish spotted with dark brown. Specimens of all sizes are powerful swimmers, and adults are rarely found far from permanent water. Juveniles are perhaps more terrestrial in habits, frequenting dry bushland and rocky terrain. Large African rock pythons prey upon animals as big as warthogs, although the diet consists in the main of smaller mammals and birds. Some 30 eggs are laid by the female in a secluded hollow or abandoned termite mound and are closely guarded until they hatch after about three months. This species is widely distributed throughout tropical Africa south of the Sahara Desert.

The **royal python** (*Python regius*) is a heavily built African species usually measuring between 3 and 6 feet in length but with a comparatively small head and short tail. The rich brown dorsal color is in marked contrast to a series of golden yellow rosettes margined with cream. The undersides are whitish. This snake is also known as the **ball python** due to its habit of coiling into a tight ball when frightened. It is primarily a terrestrial species of dry bushland and cleared forests but is also found in cultivated areas and open grassland. The female lays a small number of surprisingly large eggs from which the young hatch after about 12 weeks. Food consists mainly of rodents.

Closely related to the royal python is the **Angola python** (*Python anchietae*) of Angola and South-West Africa, a rare and secretive inhabitant of arid scrubland and rocky terrain. It attains a length of some 5 feet and feeds predominantly upon birds and small mammals.

Among those species found on the Asian continent is the **reticulated** or **regal python** (*Python reticulatus*),

Facing page: Top: *Python regius,* the royal or ball python. Photo by P. J. Stafford. Bottom: *Python anchietae,* the Angola python. Photo by Dr. W. R. Branch.

which is one of the longest of all living snakes, being reputed to reach a length of 34½ feet. The ground color varies from tan to purplish brown, over which lies a chain of dark angular markings; the head is yellowish relieved by a thin dark line. Beneath it is yellow or white. An agile snake of moderate build, the reticulated python is largely arboreal in habits but frequently descends in the vicinity of forest villages to feed upon vermin and domestic fowl. Adults are also fond of water.

The female lays a large number of eggs and, in common with most other members of this genus, incubates them for the duration of their development. The reticulated python has spread to much of Southeast Asia, including the Philippines and parts of the Indonesian archipelago.

The **black-tailed, imperial,** or **Asiatic rock python** (*Python molurus*) also ranks among the larger species, averaging between 10 and 16½ feet in length. Above it is dark brown or sometimes reddish with a complicated pattern of yellow crossbars. The flanks are conspicuously marked with rectangular blotches tinted with flecks of white and edged with black. Head coloration is dominated by a thick, dark stripe extending from the nostril past the angle of the jaw. This species is mainly terrestrial in choice of life-style but also swims and climbs readily. Most forms of warm-blooded prey are eaten. Although widely distributed throughout India and Indo-China, this species is not indigenous to Southeast Asia. Wild populations there are thought to have originated from the escaped exhibits of Indian snake charmers.

The **blood python** (*Python curtus*), also known as the

Overleaf: *Python molurus bivittatus,* the Burmese rock python, a species easily cared for in captivity. Photo by P. J. Stafford.
Facing page: The reticulated python, *Python reticulatus,* in two pattern variations. Top photo courtesy the American Museum of Natural History; bottom photo by H. Hansen, Aquarium Berlin.

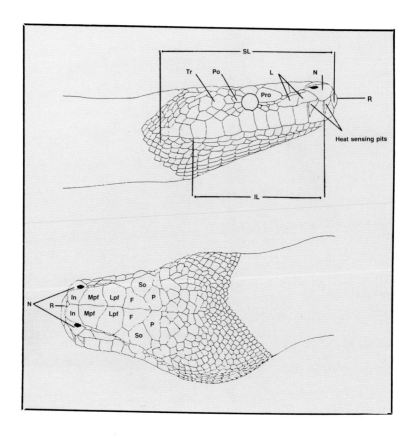

Head scales of an idealized python. F – frontal; IL – infralabials; In – internasal; L – loreal; Lpf – lateral prefrontal; Mpf – medial prefrontal; N – nasal; P – parietal; Po – postoculars; Pro – preocular; R – rostral; SL – Supralabials; So – supraocular; Tr – temporal region.

Facing page: Top: *Python molurus molurus,* the Indian rock python, is on the endangered list. Note the incomplete arrow pattern on the head (complete in *P. m. bivittatus*). Photo courtesy Cotswold Wildlife Park. **Bottom:** A large domestic specimen of *P. molurus bivittatus.* Notice how much heavier bodied this specimen is than the *Boa constrictor* partially hidden at the center. Even the most docile python or boa is potentially dangerous at this size and should always be handled with care. Photo by K. Freeman.

Head study of *Python curtus*. Art by P. J. Stafford.

short-tailed python in view of its thick and abruptly tapering tail, is a very stout species with a prominent vertebral keel. It grows to just short of 10 feet in length. The eyes are rather small in comparison to the broad head, which is red-brown, yellowish, or slate-gray in color. Overall coloration varies considerably, ranging from yellow-gray to brick red with a broken chain of brown or yellowish blotches. The ventral surface is white or pinkish suffused with gray. Being for the most part semiaquatic, the blood python inhabits swampland or dense rainforest and is most commonly seen at night awaiting prey while partially submerged in water-filled ditches, shallow pools, or at the edge of slow-moving rivers. Food consists almost entirely of small mammals and birds. The female lays from 10 to 15 eggs and remains coiled around them until hatching takes place some three months later. This species is distributed throughout southern Indo-China, Malaya, Sumatra, and Borneo.

The **Timor python** (*Python timorensis*), a rare semiarboreal species found only on the Indonesian islands of

Facing page: Two views of *Python curtus brongersmai*, the blood or short-tailed python. Photos by P. J. Stafford.

54

Timor and Flores, grows to about 10 feet in length. The head is similar in color to that of the reticulated python, but the central dark line does not extend so far forward. Dorsal coloration otherwise consists of a disorderly arrangement of dark and light brown blotches, which is perhaps more suggestive of the **amethistine python** (*Python amethistinus*) of Australia and New Guinea. This species, also referred to as the **scrub** or **Australian rock python,** attains a maximum length of about 20 feet. Coloration varies considerably throughout its range, but typical examples are olive brown above with darker transverse angular markings. The head is characterized by a dark line that descends from behind the eye to the angle of the jaw. Beneath it is whitish. The amethistine python is both terrestial and arboreal in habits, favoring dry bushland, dense rainforests, and mangrove swamps. The diet is unspecialized, consisting mainly of small mammals, birds, and large lizards. Closely allied to this species is a smaller form, the **Oenpelli** or **northern rock python** (*Python oenpelliensis*), which inhabits the rocky escarpments of northern Australia.

Boelen's python (*Python boeleni*), a shy and retiring snake from the montane forests of New Guinea, grows to a length of some 10 feet and is certainly one of the most attractive of all pythons. Above it is black with conspicuous bands of yellow extending diagonally forward from the belly; the labial scales are barred with black and yellow.

The **diamond** and **carpet pythons,** *Python spilotes,* alternatively referred to the genus *Morelia,* are but distinct color forms of a single species that occurs in Australia and New Guinea. The upper surface of the head

Facing page: Top: Close-up of the amethistine python, *Python amethistinus.* Photo by R. T. Hoser. **Bottom:** Close-up of the Oenpelli or northern rock python, *Python oenpelliensis.* Photo by R. T. Hoser.

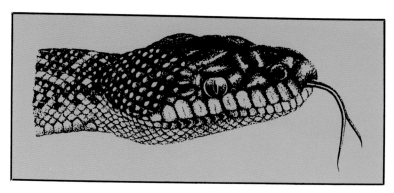

Head study of the mottled Indonesian form of *Liasis mackloti,* showing a superficial similarity to the diamond python. Art by P. J. Stafford.

is composed mainly of small, irregular sclaes rather than the large symmetrical scutes typical of most other pythons, and the head itself is more distinct from the neck. Diamond and carpet pythons grow to a length of about 10 feet and become fairly stocky when fully mature. They are mainly nocturnal and semiarboreal in habits, preferring heavily wooded areas. Food consists of small mammals, birds, and lizards. There are four subspecies in all, comprising two quite different color types. The diamond python (*Python spilotes spilotes*) varies from dark gray to light brown splashed with a multitude of bright yellow spots edged with black. The other subspccies, the carpet pythons, are characterized by yellowish blotches of varying shapes and sizes. Females of all subspecies can lay up to 40 or more eggs that take approximately ten weeks to hatch.

Bredl's or the **Centralian carpet python** (*Python bredli*), a recently described species, is similar in both proportions and coloration to the variegated forms of *Python spilotes* but is smaller and seems to be characterized by a more orderly pattern of reddish or dark brown lateral stripes and blotches.

Facing page: The diamond python, *Python spilotes spilotes.* Photos by P. J. Stafford.

INDO-AUSTRALIAN ROCK PYTHONS

Closely resembling the genus *Python* in many respects is the genus *Liasis*, represented by seven species confined to Australia, New Guinea, and parts of Indonesia. The tail is not or at most only weakly prehensile, and most of the subcaudal scales are divided.

Children's python (*Liasis childreni*) is a relatively small species of moderate build that rarely exceeds 5 feet in length. The head is pointed and wedge-shaped and the tail is somewhat shorter than in other *Liasis*. The coloration is highly variable, but typical specimens are light brown above heavily marked with darker spots and blotches. The ventral surface is white. This is one of Australia's most common pythons. It favors dry bushland, particularly those landscapes strewn with termite mounds, in which these snakes are known to take refuge. Lizards form a large part of the diet, but warm-blooded prey is also eaten. Some 15 eggs are laid in late winter or early spring and take up to four months to hatch. This python is found over much of the Australian continent and coexists in some areas with an almost identical but distinctly smaller species, the **western dwarf** or **ant hill python** (*Liasis perthensis*).

As its name implies, the **olive python** (*Liasis olivaceus*), also of Australia, is a dull olive brown in color, the undersides being white. It is a slender species about 8 feet long that is characterized by a somewhat emaciated appearance caused by the naturally ill-fitting loose folds of skin. The labial scales of the upper and lower jaws are whitish and finely dotted with gray or brown. As a rule this species is mainly terrestrial in habits, preferring rocky escarpments and river gorges of northern

Facing page: Top: A carpet python, *Python spilotes variegatus*. Photo by R. T. Hoser. **Bottom:** *Liasis perthensis*, the western dwarf python. Photo by R. T. Hoser.

and western coastal districts. It feeds upon a variety of animals, including wallabies, bushrat bandicoots, birds, and occasionally lizards. The female produces up to 40 eggs in the spring.

Four species of *Liasis* rock pythons have been recorded from New Guinea and neighboring islands, of which **D'Albert's python** *(Liasis albertisii)* is the most widespread. This small and slender species is typically an attractive bronze-brownish hue in color, fading to gray on the sides. The head and margins of the labial scales are shiny black, in sharp contrast to the whiteness of the lower jaw and remaining labial areas. In the southern part of its range dorsal coloration may be substantially darker. D'Albert's python is primarily a terrestrial species of monsoon forests and is thought to feed almost exclusively on small mammals. It grows to an average size of about 6 feet.

Macklot's python *(Liasis mackloti,* including *L. fuscus,* the Australian **water python**), a semiaquatic species, is generally restricted to the open grassy swamplands of western New Guinea but also thrives on a few neighboring islands and in northern Australia. Dorsal coloration central to the vertebrae is blackish fading to olive brown and then to gray on the sides, but some Indonesian specimens are mottled with spots of dark and light brown. The ventral surface grades from yellow under the throat to dark olive or orange-gray beneath the tail. This species grows to approximately 8 feet and subsists mainly upon small mammals, birds, and other reptiles, including juvenile crocodiles.

The **Papuan python** *(Liasis papuanus),* another fairly large terrestrial species of western New Guinea, favors

Facing page: Top: *Liasis albertisii,* D'Albert's python. Photo courtesy the Chester Zoo. **Bottom:** Macklot's python, *Liasis mackloti;* the mottled pattern is found in some Indonesian populations. Photo by P. J. Stafford.

areas of dry savannah grassland. It is very similar to the olive python *(Liasis olivaceus)*, with which it was once classified, but is distinguishable, among other characters, by the presence of black skin between the scales producing a spotted effect. The tongue, linings of the mouth, and cloaca are also deeply pigmented.

The **ringed python** *(Liasis boa)*, previously assigned to the genus *Bothrochilus*, is a rather small species rarely exceeding 5 feet in length. With the exception of New Guinea and a few other islands, it is found generally throughout the Bismarck Archipelago. Juvenile specimens are conspicuously banded with alternating rings of black and orange, but in aging examples the brighter colors may fade to dull brown or disappear altogether. In both young and old specimens the head is uniformly dark brown or blackish and the undersides are yellow. This species appears to be mostly terrestrial and feeds upon small mammals, usually by night.

GREEN TREE PYTHON

This snake represents the sole member of the genus *Chondropython* and is most distinctive in appearance. The **green tree python** *(Chondropython viridis)* is essentially arboreal in habits and has developed a strongly prehensile tail. The body is laterally compressed and the head so large as to appear completely disproportionate to the width of the body. Like the diamond and carpet pythons, to which it is most closely related, the crown of the head is covered with small, irregular scales. Adults of this species measure in the region of 6½ feet and are a vivid leaf-green flecked with blue, white, and yellow. The vertebral keel is frequently straddled by a

Facing page: Two views of the Australian water python, the *"fuscus"* form of *Liasis mackloti*. Top photo courtesy the London Zoo; bottom photo by R. T. Hoser.

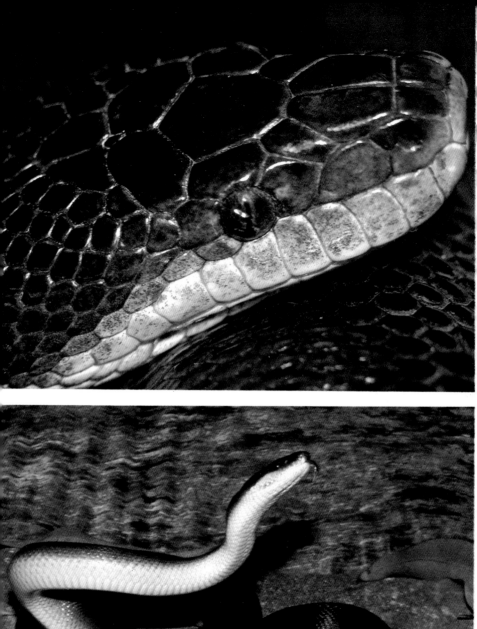

broken stripe of yellow or white. Hatchlings and juveniles under two years of age vary between bright yellow and brick red in color, also with an interrupted vertebral stripe. This species adopts an unusual resting posture among the branches shared only by a convergent group of South American tree boas *(Corallus)*. The coils are drawn into a series of folded loops, and these are neatly proportioned over a horizontal branch so that the head is always brought to rest in the center.

The green tree python feeds predominantly on birds, seizing them as they alight to roost or actively stalking them through the branches. Small mammals and tree lizards are also eaten. The female lays approximately 15 eggs on the forest floor, and within a short time of hatching the young pythons instinctively seek refuge in the trees, although adults are not generally as exclusively arboreal. The green tree python is distributed throughout New Guinea and enters northeastern Australia and the Bismarck Archipelago.

BLACK-HEADED PYTHON AND WOMA

Pythons of the genus *Aspidites* are visually distinguished from other Australian genera by an indistinct head and enlarged head scales. They are also characterized by the apparent absence of heat sensory pits, a rather inflexible jaw, and in lacking premaxillary teeth. There are two species, both of which are confined to mainland Australia and have a specialized diet consisting mainly of other reptiles, including highly venomous snakes.

Overleaf: Left page: An adult green tree python, *Chondropython viridis,* in the characteristic resting position. Photo by W. Tomey. **Right page, top:** *Chondropython viridis,* the blue phase. Photo by P. J. Stafford. **Right page, bottom:** Close-up of *Chondropython viridis.* Photo by P. J. Stafford.

The **black-headed python** (*Aspidites melanocephalus*), averaging some 8 feet in length, is creamish to brown in color and is banded with rings of dark brown or red. The head, throat, and neck are glossy black in contrast to the white undersides. Black-headed pythons show no distinct preference for any particular habitat and can be found from arid bushland to humid rainforests. Terrestrial by nature, they are also inclined to burrow, especially during hot weather. Birds, small mammals, snakes, lizards, and amphibians constitute the better part of the diet, but where this species occurs in relative abundance its own hatchlings and juveniles not infrequently fall prey to adult specimens. The average clutch contains about eight eggs, which are usually laid during the months of August and September. The species is distributed mainly in the northern third of Australia.

The **woma** or **Ramsay's python** (*Aspidites ramsayi*) is found in more southerly areas of Australia, particularly in semidesert habitats. The dorsal surface is olive, grayish, or brick red, heavily banded with darker hues. In mature or aging examples these bands are faint or sometimes absent. The head is olive or grayish brown, and the belly is yellowish with darker blotches.

Overleaf: Top: The green tree boa, *Corallus caninus*, for comparison with the green tree python. Notice especially the large and distinct scales on top of the head of the boa, while the python has very small and irregular scales. Photo by H. Hansen, Aquarium Berlin. **Bottom:** The woma or Ramsay's python, *Aspidites ramsayi*. Photo by R. T. Hoser.

Facing page: The Calabar burrowing python, *Calabaria reinhardti*. Photos by P. J. Stafford.

3: Calabariinae and Loxoceminae— Burrowing Pythons

The two remaining types of pythons are quite distinct from all others and have been placed in subfamilies of their own.

SUBFAMILY CALABARIINAE

The **Calabar burrowing python** *(Calabaria reinhardti)* of West Africa is mainly subterranean in habits. As might be expected of a burrowing snake, the body is cylindrical and of the same circumference throughout for ease of movement under the ground. Above it is a rich dark brown mottled with paler blotches that decrease in number laterally from the vertebrae. The ventral surface is also dark brown. This little python, measuring at most only 3 feet, inhabits heavily wooded areas. It tunnels under the leaf litter in search of prey. It can simultaneously asphyxiate several small rodents by simply pressing them against the walls of their burrow and consumes them afterward at its leisure. From a distance it is very difficult indeed to distinguish the head of this python from its tail, the reason for which only becomes clear when it is surprised moving above ground. The head is pressed firmly to the ground and the tail raised slightly, imitating the actions a typical snake would make with its head. In this way the attention of a predator is distracted from the real head and focused on the tail, where an injury that could otherwise be fatal is not generally so serious.

Burrowing pythons have been found some distance from the ground and apparently climb well, which is remarkable considering how specialized they have become

The Mexican burrowing python, *Loxocemus bicolor* (above). Some herpetologists feel that this snake is not a true python but instead is more
closely related to the sunbeam snakes, represented here by *Xenopeltis
unicolor* (below). Photos by Dr. S. A. Minton.

for life on and below the ground. Some captive specimens will climb readily if given the opportunity. If molested this species coils into a tight ball in much the same way as does the royal python, and it also appears to be more diurnal in habits than other pythons. Mating among captive Calabar burrowing pythons has been observed during November and December.

SUBFAMILY LOXOCEMINAE

We conclude the pythons with perhaps the most intriguing species of all, one whose geographical distribution still remains largely unexplained. The **Mexican burrowing python** (*Loxocemus bicolor*) inhabits southern Mexico and northern Central America, practically as far from all other pythons as it could possibly be. It is the only python to occur in the New World, although many herpetologists readily point out that it is not at all closely related to the Old World pythons and may have evolved in association with a completely different family of snakes, the Xenopeltidae (sunbeam snakes). It is a small burrowing species reaching approximately 3 feet in length. The head is laterally compressed and rather pointed, an adaptation for burrowing in loose earth. There is little distinction between the head and the neck, but the body is more regular in form and the tail, although short, tapers to a point. Unlike most other burrowing snakes, the eyes are quite large and vision is relatively keen. The Mexican burrowing python is dark purplish or reddish brown in color mottled with paler spots and blotches. The underparts are yellowish. It is generally collected in the lowlands of Mexico, preferring dry and rocky habitats. Specimens have been recorded south to Costa Rica. Very few observations have been made on its behavior either in the wild or in captivity, although it will often coil into a ball and hide its head among the folds if molested.

The common boa constrictor, *Boa constrictor constrictor*, with details of the dorsal pattern in the region of the tenth saddle (above left) and of the ventral pattern (above right). Photos above by J. K. Langhammer; that below by P. J. Stafford.

4: Boinae—True Boas

Boas constitute by far the greater part of the family Boidae, contesting pythons for size and diversity of forms. The subfamily Boinae contains all of the largest boas, including such fabled serpents as the anaconda and boa constrictor, neither of which, incidentally, grow to anywhere near the monstrous sizes described in some popular literature.

BOA CONSTRICTORS

The **boa constrictor** *(Boa constrictor)*, the only species of the genus *Boa* (sometimes called genus *Constrictor* in older literature), averages between 6½ and 11½ feet in length but has on occasion been known to reach over 13 feet. Dorsally the coloration is cream or brownish dominated by a series of dark saddle-like bands. Toward the tail these markings become wider and the color intensifies to a deep red-brown edged with black and cream. The flanks display irregular rhombic patterns, and the whole body, including the ventral surface, is splashed with dark spots. The boa constrictor is a very adaptable snake capable of tolerating extremely diverse conditions. Crop plantations are a favorite haunt, where it preys upon small mammals, birds, and lizards. Between 11 and 60 young are born from May to September. This species has a wide geographic range from

Facing page: Top: *Boa constrictor amarali.* Photo by Dr. M. Freiberg.
Bottom: The very dark Argentine boa, *Boa constrictor occidentalis.* Photo by Dr. M. Freiberg.

The two "red–tailed" boas. Above is the Amazonian "red–tail," found as individuals in many South American populations of *Boa constrictor constrictor.* On the facing page is *Boa constrictor melanogaster,* the black–bellied boa of Ecuador. Photos by J. K. Langhammer.

northern Mexico through Central America to northern Argentina. It also occurs in the Lesser Antilles.

ANACONDAS

The anacondas (genus *Eunectes*) from the tropics of South America are highly aquatic boas of freshwater rivers and lakes. Much the largest is the **green anaconda** (*Eunectes murinus*), which measures up to 32 feet in length. Ordinarily the ground color is greenish gray fading posteriorly to yellow. The dorsal surface is characterized by a longitudinal row of black or brownish circular blotches, and the head is flanked on both sides by a yellowish stripe margined with black. A dark spear-like marking dominates the top of the head and is always present, but dorsal coloration may vary. Underneath it is yellow or grayish with small but well-defined spots.

Anacondas move sluggishly on land. They are expert climbers but are perhaps only really at home in slow-moving rivers, where they can occasionally be seen floating with the current on mats of uprooted aquatic vegetation or fallen trees. Prey is usually seized at the water's edge and dragged underwater to be drowned and constricted. The diet includes small mammals, birds, turtles, fishes, and small caimans. Green anacondas give birth to a maximum of about 80 young.

The **yellow anaconda** (*Eunectes notaeus*) of Paraguay is similar in appearance but rarely grows to more than 10 feet in length. This species retains the dorsal blotches of its close relative, but they are smaller, more numerous, and on a ground color that is somewhat paler and more yellowish. There are two other very poorly known species of anacondas in northeastern and north-central South America.

Overleaf: The woma, *Aspidites ramsayi*. Photo by R. T. Hoser.
Facing page: Top: The green or common anaconda, *Eunectes murinus*. Photo by Dr. M. Freiberg. **Bottom:** Headstudy of the yellow anaconda, *Eunectes notaeus*. Photo courtesy the London Zoo.

TREE BOAS

Snakes of the South American genus *Corallus* (formerly *Boa*), numbering three species, are highly specialized arboreal forms distinguished by a long, slender body and large head that is well-defined from the neck. Unlike those of pythons, the heat sensing labial pits (absent in the other larger boas) are situated between and not on the labial scales.

Quite the most spectacular species is the **emerald green tree boa** *(Corallus caninus)* of northern South America, which attains some 8 feet in length. Above it is a brilliant leaf green with white or yellow vertebral blotches. The underside is yellow. This species and its pythonine equivalent, the green tree python *(Chondropython viridis)*, have evolved into almost identical forms. These snakes inhabit different parts of the world and derive from separate ancestral origins but over many thousands of years have acquired similar appearances in response to a similar way of life, a concept known as parallelism. They even share the very same resting posture among the branches.

The **garden tree boa** *(Corallus enydris)* occurs in two subspecies over much of central and northern South America. The typical race *(Corallus e. enydris)* reaches up to 8 feet in length and is grayish above with circular brown blotches edged with yellow and sometimes black. It feeds mainly upon birds and small mammals, especially bats, but the diet also includes lizards. **Cook's tree boa** *(Corallus enydris cookii)*, which occurs north of the range of the nominate form, is smaller, seldom exceeding 6½ feet in length. Its coloration is tremendously

---

Facing page: Top: *Eunectes notaeus,* the yellow anaconda. Photo by Dr. M. Frieberg. **Bottom:** A young orange-brown specimen of the green tree boa, *Corallus caninus.* Photo by J. K. langhammer.

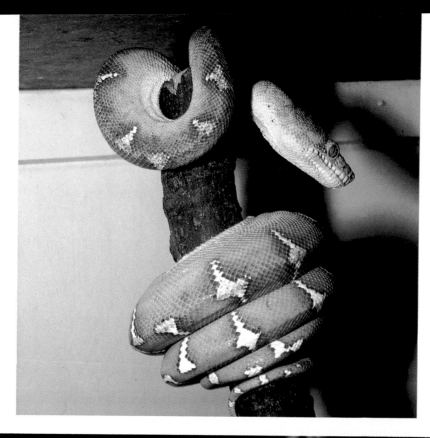

variable and ranges from orange brown to almost black, while the body may be heavily patterned or perfectly uniform. The undersides of all *C. enydris* are generally white spotted with gray. The garden tree boa has perfected a special technique in climbing trees: it stretches upward and wraps the front of its body around the trunk, whereupon the rest is then hauled up to the advanced position and reanchored, enabling the snake to reach a little higher.

In captivity, mating has been observed during the months of December and January, followed by the birth of between 7 and 30 offspring some 5 to 6 months later.

The **annulated tree boa** *(Corallus annulatus)* is a similar but more robust species averaging approximately 5 to 6½ feet in length. It is generally gray or brownish in color and is sometimes marked with indistinct lateral blotches.

RAINBOW AND WEST INDIAN BOAS

Boas of the genus *Epicrates* are small to medium-sized snakes of semiarboreal habits. There are 10 species total, all but one of which are restricted to the West Indies. This group may at some point be redefined to incorporate the genus *Xenoboa*, whose only species (from South America) is thought to be a close relative.

The **rainbow boa** *(Epicrates cenchria)* is a rather stocky snake measuring at most only 5 feet. It occurs in

nine subspecies distributed through continental South America and southern Central America from Costa Rica to northern Argentina. Quite the most familiar form to collectors is the widespread Colombian race, *E. c. maurus*, which is typically brownish above with an irregular series of faint ocellate blotches. The rainbow boa appears to be more terrestrial than other *Epicrates*, favoring cultivated land, forest edges, and rocky locations. Prey consists mainly of small mammals, birds, and lizards. Only the nominate subspecies (*E. c. cenchria*) has iridescent colors that justify the description implied by its common name.

The **Cuban boa** (*Epicrates angulifer*) is the largest species of the genus, measuring up to 10 feet in length. Dorsal coloration varies from yellow-brown to grayish complemented by an irregular series of dark angular markings. Beneath it is yellowish with gray under the tail. The Cuban boa is essentially arboreal in habits, preferring woodland, rocky slopes, and caves. Bats form a substantial part of the diet, but other small mammals and birds are taken with equal enthusiasm. This species is widespread on Cuba but also extends to several neighboring islands. It is rather irritable in captivity and will strike at the slightest provocation. Cuban boas are fairly active snakes and should be provided with spacious accommodations.

Ford's boa (*Epicrates fordii*), a smallish boid measuring about 3 feet in length, is generally pale brown or gray in color with numerous contrasting darker blotches and spots that may form a chain-like pattern. The ventral surface is white suffused with gray. This boa, indig-

enous to the Dominican Republic, is primarily an inhabitant of xeric scrubland, sheltering in small bushes, grassy tussocks, and among the entangled dry foliage on the trunks of palm trees. It feeds predominantly on small mammals and lizards. A similar species, the **vine boa** *(Epicrates gracilis)* occurs in the same localities but is a more slender snake than *E. fordii* and has a strongly compressed body. Coloration of the dorsal surface is also somewhat darker.

Fischer's boa *(Epicrates striatus)* is distributed in the form of eight subspecies over much of the Caribbean, found only on specific islands and nowhere else. It grows to an average length of between 5 and 6½ feet. Typical specimens are pale yellow-brown or red-brown heavily blotched with dark rectangular markings edged with black. The underside is gray spotted with dark brown. Cacao and banana groves are favorite haunts, but these boas are equally abundant in natural woodland, hunting small mammals, birds, and lizards usually at night.

The **Jamaican boa** *(Epicrates subflavus)* and the **Puerto Rican boa** *(Epicrates inornatus)* are in many ways similar to the preceding species and are equally as variable in coloration. Both are fairly large, rapacious snakes reaching 6½ feet or more in length. Although they can be kept successfully in captivity, they are usually aggressive by nature and difficult to handle.

PACIFIC ISLAND BOAS

Other boas that appear rather sensitive in captivity include those of the genus *Candoia* from the South Pacific islands. These attractively marked snakes (often called

Facing page: Top: Close-up of the Cuban boa, *Epicrates angulifer.* **Bottom:** Close-up of Fischer's boa, *Epicrates striatus striatus.* Photos by P. J. Stafford.

Solomons boas or Fiji boas) are unusual in as much as all the dorsal scales are keeled rather than only partially so or totally smooth as with most other boids. Pacific island boas are characterized by angulate snouts and slightly compressed bodies. Their tails are short and prehensile. They are found mainly in areas of dense forest but also frequent cultivated land, feeding upon small mammals, birds, lizards, and frogs. They give birth to 20 or more offspring. There are three species, of which the **rough-scaled Pacific island boa** *(Candoia carinata)* is the most widespread. This snake grows to over 3 feet in length and is typically pale brown, gray, or reddish brown above with a darker zig-zag pattern extending the entire length of the body and straddling the vertebrae. Beneath it is white or gray peppered with fine dark spots. *Candoia carinata* is primarily terrestrial in habits, sheltering under fallen logs, rocks, or leaf litter during the day.

Bibron's Pacific island boa *(Candoia bibroni)* is a larger species reaching 6½ feet in length. Its coloration is highly variable, consisting normally of irregular gray and brown blotches that may fuse at the vertebral ridge to form a zig-zag pattern, but never so well-defined as in *Candoia carinata*. This species is mainly arboreal and is an efficient climber.

Overleaf: Left page: Top: *Epicrates inornatus,* the Puerto Rican boa. Photo by Dr. S A. Minton. **Left page: Bottom:** Ford's boa, *Epicrates fordii fordii.* Photo by P. J. Stafford. **Right page:** Fischer's boa, *Epicrates striatus.* Photo by J. Dodd.

Facing page: Top: The rough-scaled Pacific island boa, *Candoia carinata.* **Bottom:** The Madagascan tree boa, *Sanzinia madagascariensis.* Photos courtesy the Chester Zoo.

MADAGASCAN BOAS

Curious though it may seem, Madagascar is the home of several animals whose nearest relatives occur not in neighboring Africa as one might expect but much further afield in continental South America. This is also true of three kinds of boa assigned to the genera *Acrantophis* and *Sanzinia*.

Dumeril's boa (*Acrantophis dumerili*) and the **Madagascan boa constrictor** (*Acrantophis madagascariensis*) are closely allied to the common boa constrictor of Central and South America. They grow to roughly the same size and share similar markings, consisting of an intricate pattern of dark and light dorsal blotches. These snakes are mainly terrestrial in habits and their diet is unspecialized, comprising almost any animal of suitable size.

The **Madagascan tree boa** (*Sanzinia madagascariensis*), an attractive species adapted to life in the trees, has acquired an appearance similar to that of the South America tree boas of the genus *Corallus*. This species measures approximately 6½ feet when fully grown and is grayish brown or olive-brown in color with dark circular blotches decorating the flanks. The head is grayish, with a prominent dark stripe extending from the eye past the angle of the jaws.

Facing page: The exquisitely beautiful Dumeril's boa, *Acrantophis dumerili*. Photo by K. Lucas at Steinhart Aquarium.

5: Erycinae—Ground Boas

This group comprises three genera of small terrestrial and semifossorial snakes. The first two, *Lichanura* and *Charina*, each contain a single species and occupy the most northerly range of all boids, extending well into the temperate latitudes of western North America.

NORTHERN BOAS

The **rubber boa** *(Charina bottae)* grows to approximately 3 feet in length. The tail is shaped like the head and is habitually presented in the face of danger while the real head is hidden below the coils (much as in *Calabaria)*. Coloration is consistently gray or brown above and more yellowish beneath, sometimes with a peppering of gray flecks on the lower sides; juveniles are usually paler. The eyes are small, and the crown of the head is composed of fairly large symmetrical plates. This species is not particular in its choice of habitat and can be found in coniferous or deciduous forests, grassland, under fallen timbers, or in piles of rubbish. It is adapted mainly to a fossorial way of life but also climbs and swims admirably. Food consists of small mammals and lizards. Between one and eight offspring are born in late

Overleaf: The rubber boa, *Charina bottae.* Photo by K. Lucas at Steinhart Aquarium.
Facing page: A rosy boa, *Lichanura trivirgata.* Photo by K. Lucas at Steinhart Aquarium.

summer. This is the most northerly of the boas, being found in much of the Pacific Northwest of the United States, the northern Rocky Mountains area, and parts of southwestern Canada.

The **rosy boa** (*Lichanura trivirgata*) measures between 2 and 4 feet in length and has a short tail and small head. The coloration varies from pale gray-brown to red-brown above, with three darker stripes (often irregular) extending the entire length of the body. The underside is cream, spotted with gray or brown. This small ground boa inhabits rocky bushland and scrub, always residing within reach of water. It is a good climber and not in the least averse to scaling precarious slopes or small trees in pursuit of birds, lizards, and small mammals. Copulation takes place in late spring, the female giving birth to between five and ten offspring in the autumn. The rosy boa inhabits the drier areas of northwestern Mexico and the southwestern United States.

SAND BOAS

Boas of the genus *Eryx* (10 species) are predominantly fossorial in habits and live mainly in hot, sandy regions of northern and eastern Africa, southeastern Europe, and Asia. They are able to tolerate wide extremes of temperature and can withstand long periods of drought. The head is blunt, wedge-shaped, and covered with granular scales. Some species lack a mental groove (the longitudinal depression under the chin between the middle scale rows). While generally sluggish in movements, these snakes are quick to bite, seizing prey in a sudden and rapid sidelong strike.

Facing page: Top: *Eryx jaculus,* the European spotted sand boa. **Bottom:** *Eryx tataricus.* Photos by Dr. S. A. Minton.

The **European javelin** or **spotted sand boa** *(Eryx jaculus)* rarely exceeds 30 inches in length and averages considerably less. Dorsal coloration is usually grayish, brown, or reddish brown with darker bars and blotches that may form a vertebral chain. There is often a dark arrow-like marking on the nape. Beneath it is yellow or white. This species feeds upon small rodents, birds, and lizards, seizing them from just below the surface or actively hunting them above the ground at night. If unearthed during the day they are lethargic and slow to respond but become very much more alert as night falls. The European sand boa gives birth to a litter of between six and 18 offspring. It occurs in southeastern Europe (including several of the Greek islands), southwestern Asia, and northern Africa.

The **rough-scaled sand boa** *(Eryx conicus)* grows to much the same size as the preceding species. Coloration of the dorsal surface is also similar, but the markings are usually bolder and often fuse along the vertebral line to produce a viper-like zig-zag pattern. The scales are weakly keeled in the region of the neck and trunk but become enlarged and distinctly coarser posteriorly. The undersurface is white or yellowish. This sand boa is found mainly in arid districts of India, Pakistan, and Sri Lanka. Between one and 11 offspring are produced in each litter.

Also from India is the **brown** or **blunt-tailed sand boa** *(Eryx johnii)*. This species is brownish in color and grows to a length of some 30 inches. The young are distinctly banded. It is not quite as stout in appearance as

Facing page: **Top:** The Kenyan sand boa, *Eryx colubrinus loveridgei*. Photo by P. J. Stafford. **Bottom:** The brown sand boa, *Eryx johnii johnii*. Photo by J. P. Swaak.

Eryx conicus, but the tail is even more blunt and is often used to confuse an enemy in the same manner as noted in *Calabaria* and *Charina*.

Mueller's sand boa (*Eryx muelleri*) of Africa is one of the smallest species of the genus, averaging less than 15 inches in length. Above it is pale orange or yellow-brown patterned with darker irregular blotches. In common with most other sand boas, it favors dry, sandy areas, especially along the perimeters of deserts, where it feeds upon small mammals and lizards.

Jayakar's sand boa (*Eryx jayakari*) from the sandy wastes of Arabia and the Middle East is another small species measuring approximately 15 inches in length. The eyes are very small and positioned entirely on the upper surface of the head, enabling it to lie in the sand and wait for prey with little else visible to reveal its identity. This sand boa is grayish or yellow-brown above speckled with white and traversed with irregular cross bands of dark brown.

Facing page: The brown sand boa, *Eryx johnii*. The specimen at the bottom is a juvenile with distinct bands. Photo above by G. Marcuse; that below by Dr. S. A. Minton.

A juvenile rough-scaled sand boa, *Eryx conicus.* Photo by P. J. Stafford.

6: Tropidophiinae and Bolyeriinae—Dwarf Boas

Despite the retention of some primitive features, boas of the last two subfamilies possess more characters associated with higher snakes than do any other subfamilies of the family Boidae.

SUBFAMILY TROPIDOPHIINAE

This subfamily contains four genera of little-known boas that differ from others by the presence of a well-developed tracheal lung and in having lost most of the left lung. Moreover, the females of some species assigned to this subfamily have lost all traces of the pelvic spurs.

The **wood snakes** (genus *Tropidophis*) number 15 species with 16 additional subspecies, most of which inhabit the Caribbean islands, where they represent what is perhaps the dominant group of indigenous snakes. They range from about 12 inches to over 3 feet in length and prefer rocky, cavernous localities, coming out at night to hunt small lizards upon which they prey almost exclusively. Their tails are prehensile but short, and the body is cylindrical to slightly compressed. Wood snakes resort to what could be described as one of the most drastic of all defensive measures adopted by snakes. After coiling into a tight ball, the eyes become heavily stained with blood and the roof of the mouth also begins to bleed alarmingly. This is accompanied by the simultaneous expulsion of an obnoxious scent from a pair of glands at the base of the tail.

These snakes vary considerably in color and pattern. *T. melanurus* from Cuba is pale yellowish or gray speck-

Tropidophis greenwayi. A Bahamian wood snake. Photo by Dr. S. A. Minton.

led with dark, yellow-centered spots and on each side of the body there are two dark longitudinal stripes. In *T. taczanowskyi*, from Amazonian northwestern South America, the lower parts are black and yellow while the dorsal surface is brownish, heavily marked with large black spots. Another Cuban species, *T. pardalis*, is characterized by a dark transverse crossbar on the snout and yellowish underparts spotted with brown.

Tropidophis species are among the most advanced snakes of the family Boidae, as noticeably reflected in the character and arrangement of the scales, which are more suggestive of higher snakes than of other boas.

Boas of the genus *Trachyboa* (two species), sometimes called **spiny boas,** are small, stout snakes with short and stocky tails. They are essentially terrestrial in habits, favoring the humid lowland forests of northern South America and southern Central America. Dorsal coloration consists in the main of an irregular series of lusterless brown blotches that provide concealment on the forest floor, where they forage for food. *Trachyboa gularis* also has two alternating series of black spots on each side of the body and yellowish ventrals. The dorsal scales of both species are strongly ridged and are upturned on the head giving the appearance of sharp spines.

The genus *Ungaliophis*, once called the **banana boas** because occasional specimens were found in shipments of bananas in northern ports, also contains two species that occur in Central America and northern South America. They are immediately distinguished from other boas of this subfamily by the presence of an oversized single internasal scale that dominates the upper surface of the head. These boas are generally slender in build and lead a secretive nocturnal life. *Ungaliophis panamensis*, a light-colored species with contrasting darker ovoid blotches, is thought to be largely arboreal, having been encountered aloft in banana plantations where it probably feeds upon small lizards and treefrogs. *U. continentalis* from Central America is pale brown or grayish with a series of yellow-edged black spots on the back. A dark stripe extends from each nostril to the eyes, and the lower parts are speckled with black and yellow. Both species grow to a maximum length of approximately 3 feet.

The cool montane cloud forests of southern Mexico seem an unlikely place to find a snake of any sort but provide a suitable environment for the **Oaxacan boa,** genus *Exiliboa*, which, so far as is known, occurs only

Facing page: **Top:** *Tropidophis haetianus haetianus;* a preserved specimen. **Bottom:** *Tropidophis semicinctus;* a preserved specimen. Photos by P. J. Stafford.

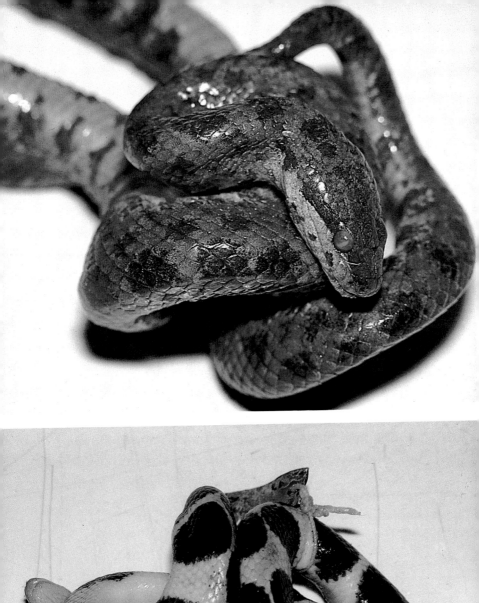

in these high altitude forests and in no other habitat. A single species has been described, *E. placata*. This snake is almost completely black in color with a highly polished iridescent skin. The tail is prehensile but apparently of little value, for this small boa appears to be predominantly fossorial in habits, subsisting upon frogs and perhaps other amphibians found in abundance under rocks and fallen timber where it lives.

SUBFAMILY BOLYERIINAE

The **Round Island boa** and **keel-scaled boa,** from Round Island off Mauritius in the southern Indian Ocean, comprise two species each contained in different genera, *Bolyeria* and *Casarea*. Both forms (sometimes collectively called Round Island boas) have suffered considerably at the hands of rats and feral domestic animals that arrived with the first settlers. Much of the original landscape of the little island has now disappeared, leaving behind a stony and sparsely vegetated environment in which the remaining population of these boas can barely survive, let alone prosper. Round Island boas are medium-sized snakes of slender build, a feature that might easily be misinterpreted as an adaptation to an arboreal way of life. *Bolyeria* also has a long tapering tail but in spite of this appears to be largely fossorial in habits, using its snout to shovel through loose earth. While both species have strongly keeled dorsal scales, they differ significantly in the number of ventral and subcaudal scales. The left lung is greatly reduced and the pelvic girdle and spurs, so characteristic of most boids, are absent in both sexes.

Facing page: Top: A spiny boa, *Trachyboa boulengeri;* a preserved specimen. **Bottom:** A banana boa, *Ungaliophis panamensis;* a preserved specimen. Photos by P. J. Stafford.

7: Captive Breeding

Although concern for the preservation of wildlife in general has escalated during recent years, snakes as a group have received little beneficial publicity. This aspect of keeping pythons and boas is therefore of paramount importance for it presents a means of conservation in which the amateur can actively participate.

MATING

The successful inducement of reproduction in captive snakes is more or less dependent on being able to produce the right set of conditions at the right time of the year.

The simplest way of determining the sex of a boid is to count the number of paired or single subcaudal scales (*i.e.*, those on the underside between the vent and the tip of the tail). Males usually possess a greater number than females and a correspondingly lower number of ventral scales. The enthusiast must first, however, determine the average counts for the species in question by checking the appropriate literature to have a basis for comparison.

Many snake breeders prefer to have their animals mechanically probed to determine the sex. This is an accurate but delicate operation that should only be per-

Facing page: **Top:** Few boids have externally obvious sexual characters, so advanced breeders often prefer to have their snakes probed to determine sex. This method has its dangers and disadvantages, however. Photo by J. Gee. **Bottom:** Standardized housing makes regular care of snakes easier and thus leads to healthier snakes that are more likely to breed in captivity. Photo by R. W. Applegate.

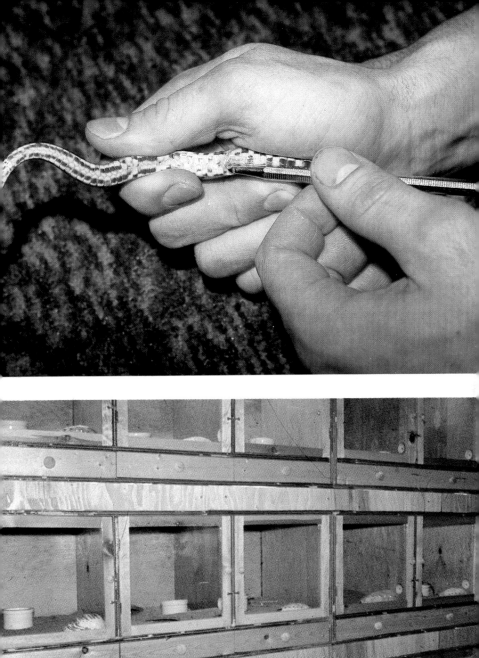

formed by an experienced herpetologist who is aware of the consequences of error. A lubricated rod is gently inserted into the vent toward the tip of the tail. Should the snake be a male, the instrument will pass to a length of at least eight subcaudals into one of the hemipenile pockets on either side of the tail. In females it usually will not pass more than three, if at all. Caution should again be emphasized, for the use of force can easily result in injury. Even this method is not absolutely foolproof, as the probe can sometimes be passed to lengths of greater than three subcaudals in the females of some species.

It is widely accepted that the female becomes receptively fertile only at certain times of the year, simultaneously producing a scent to which males are sexually attracted. Periods of female fertility generally coincide in equatorial regions with seasonal cooling and can sometimes be determined in captivity by half-hearted at-

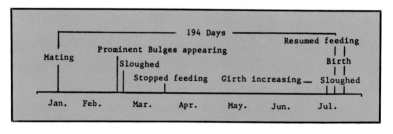

Record of gestation in a captive female Cook's tree boa, *Corallus enydris cookii.*

Facing page: Top: Copulation in the woma, *Aspidites ramsayi.* The cloacas of the specimens are in contact on top of the rock in the foreground. **Bottom:** Incubation of eggs by *Liasis perthensis,* the western dwarf python. Notice the comparatively large size of the eggs. Photos by R. T. Hoser.

tempts at courtship. Vigorous mating behavior can often be aroused by cooling the male for a number of days or weeks; in fact, this is believed to be necessary for the achievement of spermatogenesis. Under captive conditions this should be simulated by allowing the temperature at night to fall to between 70° and 75° F. Daytime temperatures should hover around 80° F. Mating usually takes place during the rainy season, which generally corresponds to winter and early spring in temperate latitudes. Again the exact time varies considerably among species and individuals.

Some snake-breeders artificially control the hours of daylight and darkness, pursuing the theory that a gradual increase in day length and temperature (simulating the environmental conditions of spring) encourages many animals to breed. This has proved especially true of diurnal snakes, but as most tropical boids are naturally exposed to equal amounts of both daylight and darkness, it can be assumed that this is not essential to induce courtship.

Many authorities recommend separating the sexes prior to attempts at breeding. Indeed, copulation can often be elicited by employing this strategy alone. Some males display a greater incentive to copulate when reintroduced to the female after a short period of isolation. Alternatively, a single female can be presented to a party of males, creating natural competition.

Copulation usually takes place during twilight hours and at night. The male assumes the dominant role, manipulating his body into a series of random loops over his mate. Should the female be enthusiastic, she will respond by raising her tail slightly, exposing the cloaca.

Facing page: Several methods have been developed to incubate python and other snake eggs, and all have their followers. The photo at top shows eggs incubating in a tray of vermiculite. That at the bottom shows *Python regius* eggs hatching on damp paper towels. Photo at top by J. Gee; that at bottom by R. W. Applegate.

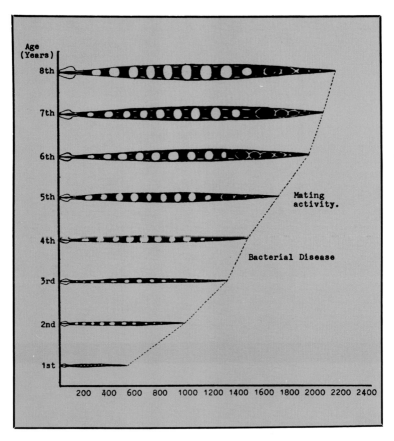

Rate of growth in a captive female boa constrictor *Boa constrictor constrictor*. Many factors affect the rate of growth of captive boas and pythons.

Facing page: Anything that saps the strength of captive boids may result in their not breeding in captivity even if other conditions are excellent. If large numbers of parasites are present they may interfere with breeding. **Top:** *Polydelphis,* a nematode from *Python molurus.* **Bottom:** Cross section of an *Amblyomma* tick in the skin of a snake; notice the barbed mouthparts. Photos by Dr. E. Elkan.

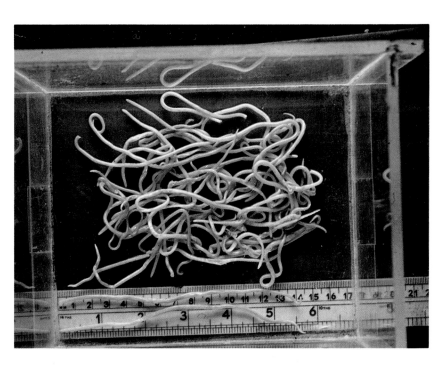

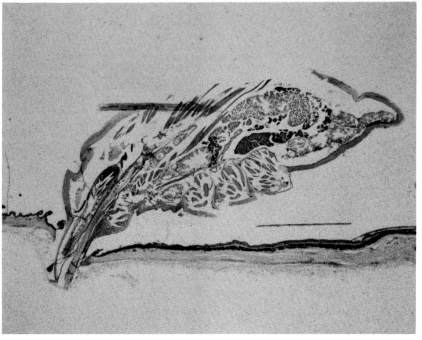

127

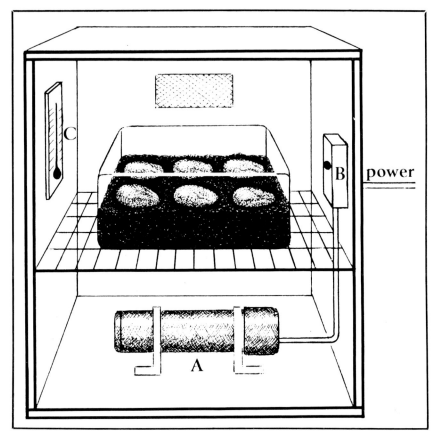

A simple incubator constructed from chipboard, complete with heater (A), thermostat (B), and thermometer (C). The eggs are placed in a separate container to maintain high humidity. Access can be through the front panel (removed in this illustration). Art by P. J. Stafford.

During frenzied acts of courtship the male maintains intimate contact with the female and may be totally oblivious of attempts to distract his attention. Although both sexes (with rare exceptions) possess pelvic spurs, those of the male are usually larger and are frequently used during courtship to excite the female by rhythmically stroking her flanks. Actual copulation is completed by the insertion of the male hemipene into the cloaca of the female, followed by the release of sperm. Copulation may be a much simpler procedure than that described. Sexually aroused snakes may dispense with preliminary courtship behavior and simply lie in an entangled coil with the tails coupled. In snakes that are exclusively nocturnal, mating behavior may easily pass unnoticed. Should this be suspected, close examination of the substrate and vivarium furnishings may reveal "misplaced" semen deposits.

Copulation can last from a few minutes to several hours. A successful attempt will be confirmed in the female by a gradual increase in girth, during which time she may refuse to feed. Egg-laying in pythons occurs approximately two to three months from the date of copulation and is usually preceded by a final shed. Boas usually give birth between five and six months after mating. Toward the appointed time the female becomes noticeably restless, sometimes pressing her snout into crevices or corners of the cage as if attempting to burrow. When this is observed egg-laying or birth is very close indeed, and the female will appreciate a hiding box for privacy.

These guidelines do not offer a guaranteed recipe for success in breeding pythons and boas, but instead present an idealized "procedure of conduct" from which the individual may prefer to deviate. The serious breeder must be patient and self-disciplined, for only by experimenting will he eventually discover the right combination of conditions under which his particular snakes will breed.

INCUBATION OF PYTHON EGGS
Soon after the eggs are laid, they tightly adhere to each other and become very difficult to separate without tearing the shells. If this happens the keeper may prefer to leave the female to her own devices, providing she is willing. The majority of snake-breeders, however, favor

artificial means of incubation for they offer a greater control of the situation and therefore a better chance of hatching the eggs successfully.

Almost any type of household container can be converted into an ideal incubator providing it will retain heat and accommodate the size and number of eggs expected. In a more or less standard arrangement, a flat wooden box is used. Heating is provided by a low-wattage tubular heater, light bulb, or heat tape installed in such a position as to supply an even distribution of heat. The temperature is regulated by means of a thermostat mounted on the side. The eggs themselves are placed in a smaller receptacle suspended on a grid within the incubator. A plastic sandwich box is ideal for this, but any clean, moisture-retaining container will suffice. The eggs should be partially buried in a dampened, preferably sterile, medium such as styrofoam, paper towels, or vermiculite. Natural materials (*i.e.*, peat and sphagnum mosses) have produced good results, but the percentage of eggs lost through fungal infection is generally higher.

The time taken for python eggs to hatch is primarily influenced by temperature. Too high or low a temperature will almost certainly result in a high failure rate or produce hatchlings with varying degrees of deformity. The optimum temperature range for incubation lies between 85° and 90° F at a relative humidity level of between 90 and 100%. Under these conditions the eggs can be expected to hatch some 50 to 75 days after they are laid. Eggs that are discolored and flaccid are usually infertile and should be removed so as not to threaten the development of healthy embryos, but if the keeper is at all hesitant about their true condition they should be given the benefit of the doubt.

At the time of hatching, young pythons will often remain hidden inside the egg after rupturing the shell with the egg tooth. The keeper should not be too hasty

At the moment all boas and pythons are under at least nominal protection by Western governments, making imported specimens of most species difficult to obtain. Some species or subspecies, such as the Indian rock python, *Python molurus molurus,* shown above, may become available strictly in the form of specimens bred in captivity. Photo by G. Marcuse.

to lend a helping hand, for all baby snakes need some time to adjust. Some breeders systematically slit all the remaining eggs after the first has hatched for fear of losing a baby through suffocation should it be unable to break the shell and escape. This may be advisable if the first hatchling experiences unexpected difficulties.

8: The Care of Boids in Captivity

While this section is primarily concerned with keeping the larger constrictors in captivity, the guidelines presented apply to most species of snakes and, indeed, the majority of reptiles as a whole. Of all the reptiles, pythons and boas appear to be the most popular among enthusiasts, no doubt in part because of the impressive size attained by some species and their attractive coloration. It would be wrong, however, to look upon these animals as affectionate pets and quite unprofessional to approach the subject from anything other than a practical, scientific point of view.

HOUSING

When designing an enclosure for the purpose of housing a reptile of any description, the habits of the species to be accommodated must always be of first and foremost consideration. There would, after all, be little point in providing a tree-dwelling lizard or snake with a vivarium that would be more suited to a species adapted for life on or below the ground. Serious thought should also be given to the number of specimens the cage is to house and, last but not least, provision for the size they are expected to reach.

The vivarium must be able to efficiently maintain the appropriate temperature and humidity and must be easy to clean and repair. Glass aquaria seem to be widely used as they are easy to clean and come in all shapes and sizes. The main drawbacks are that for the dimensions required to accommodate large species they are heavy, poor retainers of heat, and often expensive to buy. Excessive condensation collection on the inside can also lead to respiratory complications if the aquaria are inadequately ventilated. Wood is generally a good material with which to build a vivarium, but some types are prone to distorting under prolonged periods of heat combined with high humidity. This effect, however, can be reduced by sealing the surface with varnish or paint. Plywood is another possibility but it is rather flimsy in comparison to regular wood and needs a rigid frame for support. Probably the most suitable material is particleboard, particularly when faced with melamine or similar plastic. In addition to being relatively inexpensive, strong, and exceptionally heat-retaining, it has the added advantage of a tough, easily cleaned surface.

Whichever material is chosen, the dimensions should match as far as possible the ecological needs of the occu-

An enclosure suitable for terrestrial and semi-aquatic species. A tubular heating element located under the grid in the foreground effectively heats the air, floor, and pool to their required temperatures and also prevents condensation from forming on the sliding glass panels. Art by P. J. Stafford.

A suitable cage for arboreal species. Heat is supplied by a reflector lamp separated from the dwelling area by a screen of wire mesh. The lamp box is removable. Access is principally through the sliding glass panels at the front, but a withdrawable floor can be incorporated for ease of cleaning. Art by P. J. Stafford.

pant. Tree boas (*Corallus*), for example, appreciate a deep cage incorporating ample climbing branches, but ground-dwelling species require a longer and wider vivarium making full use of available floor space. The exact size is dependent upon the nature and potential size of the snakes in question.

Each new acquisition should be allowed to explore and become accustomed to its new surroundings with the minimum of disturbance, but perhaps more importantly, all captive snakes, regardless of how easily they may adapt, should be provided with a means of seclusion such as a hollow log or even a cardboard box into which they can withdraw if disturbed.

FURNISHING THE VIVARIUM

The decision whether to use natural or artificial materials with which to decorate a vivarium is rather a controversial matter. The whole argument revolves principally around a question of hygiene and whether or not a clinical as opposed to a natural environment affects the customary habits of the animal interned. Both points of view can be substantiated, but whichever is favored, each vivarium must include a pool of water in which the snake can totally immerse itself and some means of seclusion. Arboreal boids on the whole prefer a clump of entangled branches suspended above the floor or an elevated hiding box attached to the wall, but terrestrial species appreciate a confined space into which they can squeeze, such as a hollow log or an artificial cavern molded of fiberglass, plaster, or cement. Sand boas (*Eryx*) and other burrowing species should be provided with a deep layer of dry leaves, peat, gravel, or crushed bark, or with access to an underfloor retreat.

Green foliage, excluding cacti and some succulents, rarely survives long in a heated vivarium due to the lack of sunlight and improper humidity. Plastic imitations

The choice of such cage factors as floor covering, lighting, and temperature of course depends on the species to be kept. A green tree python (above) would require very different maintenance conditions than a small anaconda (below) . Much can be said for use of newspaper as an all-around floor covering and the use of incandescent bulbs to provide selective heating. Photos by K. Lucas at Steinhart Aquarium.

can be used instead, but authentic-looking examples are often rather expensive. Loose rocks, ivy trailers, pieces of cork bark, and dried clumps of moss are just a few other suggestions that may appeal.

The choice of floor covering should also be given careful consideration. Soil, peat, and leaf litter mixtures are likely to contain an assortment of parasites and require changing frequently. Sand is a poor substrate as it will cause undue irritation and possibly infection if particles become trapped under the scales or in the nostrils; sand can also cause serious internal problems such as peritonitis if accidentally ingested. Gravel is a more suitable medium, but in large quantities it is heavy and laborious to clean. Smaller particles should be avoided as they can cause the same problems experienced with sand. Probably the most practical solution is newspaper. This has proved an ideal substrate for it is absorbent, inexpensive to replace, and also inhibits the growth of bacteria. Although somewhat unsightly, it can be concealed with a liberal scattering of dry leaves or moss.

HEATING AND LIGHTING

All pythons and boas require a high temperature range if they are to remain healthy and active in captivity. To produce this the keeper will need to install a suitable means of heating. Ordinary incandescent light bulbs are probably one of the simplest forms available. They have been used very successfully by some enthusiasts, yet others are adamant in the belief that a relentless continuity of bright light affects the natural habits of vivarium herpetofauna. This has been particularly noticeable among nocturnal species such as boids, for example. Colored light bulbs are an improvement. Red ones should be used as they produce a comparatively lower level of white light although they may still emit sufficient light to deter some species from venturing out at

Simple cages are often the most effecient to maintain and best for the snake in the long run. Small burrowers such as *Eryx conicus* (above) can be kept in relatively small, barren, gravel-bottomed terraria with rocks for basking. The very large pythons and boas, such as the *Python reticulatus* below, need a moderately roomy (smaller than you'd think) bare cage where the heat and humidity can be controlled. Photo above by G. Marcuse; that below by K. Lucas at Steinhart Aquarium.

night. Alternatively, heating pads or tapes buried under the substrate can be used in conjunction with light bulbs to supplement the heat during the day. At night the bulbs can be switched off and the pads allowed to produce all the heat.

The author has found tubular electrical heaters such as those used in greenhouses to be the most efficient means of heating a large vivarium. Although initially expensive to buy, in the long term they are more economical to operate, especially when controlled by a thermostat. They also provide the necessary period of darkness.

Some enthusiasts have successfully used electric fan-operated space heaters to heat large vivaria. Under normal circumstances, however, the atmosphere created by these is usually too dry. While carefully controlled moisture is by no means necessary for the husbandry of many species, some boids have shown a greater incentive to reproduce when subjected to a high level of humidity. Should the keeper wish to experiment, an ample humidity can be maintained by occasionally spraying the cage and its contents with water. Emphasis must be placed on "occasionally," for continual dampness encourages respiratory and skin infections.

Many herpetologists prefer to heat the entire room in which the snakes are housed. Kerosene heaters (where legal) or electric radiators can be used, supplemented during the day by light bulbs or spot lights installed in each separate cage. Reflective spot lights are particularly efficient, directing their heat energy toward the floor of the vivarium and thus providing a "hot-spot" under which the snakes can bask. Lamps and bulbs should project from the lid and not the walls for obvious reasons.

Fluorescent tubes are another interesting idea, especially those that emit ultraviolet light. Sophisticated

The staple food for virtually all common boids is small rodents or chicks. Animals the size of the reticulated python below will take rodents up to the size of a rabbit or guinea pig. The anaconda (above) is unusual in that it will take fish, in keeping with its aquatic habit; it will not turn down rabbits, however. Photo above by L. Van der Meid; that below by G. Marcuse.

means of illuminating the vivarium are unnecessary, however, as most pythons and boas become active only when it becomes dark.

All heating elements should be protected with a screen of wire mesh or, ideally, removed completely from the dwelling area. They should also be controlled by a thermostat to prevent overheating. The optimum temperature range for keeping virtually all types of pythons and boas lies between 75° F at night and 85° F during the day.

FOOD

Snakes are carnivorous animals that as a rule feed only upon whole and intact items of prey. This is an essential that must be provided for if these reptiles are to be kept satisfactorily in captivity. Most of the species described in the preceding chapters will readily accept small mammals and birds, and some will eat other reptiles. Laboratory-bred mice, rats, and rabbits are an ideal source of the majority but should be given sparingly for they sometimes possess abnormal accumulations of fat. It should always be remembered that overfeeding in adult snakes can quickly lead to obesity and premature death.

The feeding of live animals to snakes has long been a considerable cause for concern among herpetologists. In addition to the moral aspects involved, there may also be legal issues in some areas. Many species actually prefer dead prey, and whenever possible this should be given. Should an occasion arise where it is necessary to offer live food to a snake that, despite all efforts, steadfastly refuses anything else, the snake must never be left unattended with a rodent for these animals have been known to retaliate with serious consequences. Rejected commercially hatched chicks are ideal for those species that naturally prey upon birds. Wild animals are best

Pythons and boas are often erratic in their feeding behavior. One of the worst offenders is the ball python, *Python regius* (below), but the problem is also found in most other species, including the Australian pythons such as *Python spilotes* (above). Photo above by G. Marcuse; that below by K. Lucas at Steinhart Aquarium.

avoided as they may harbor diseases and possibly contain harmful insecticides.

The amount of food given depends entirely upon the size and nature of the species in question. A large python, for example, would require a substantial meal perhaps every other week, but a juvenile should be fed more frequently on one or two mice weekly. If fed correctly, a typical adult boid should be firm to the touch and appear generally rounded. With a few exceptions, the vertebrae should be just recognizable under a little applied finger pressure, the fat deposits on either side not obscuring the spine. The appearance of loose folds of skin and projecting ribs indicates either gross underfeeding or poor health.

Many wild-caught snakes and occasionally even long-term captives have the disturbing habit of refusing to feed for considerable periods of time. A notorious example is the royal python *(Python regius)* of western Africa, although many other species habitually adopt this procedure. Such behavior may coincide with a natural period of fasting but is more usually caused by stress incurred during capture or transportation. It is sometimes a condition that is very difficult to reverse and is always a cause of anxiety to the owner. One method that has proved very successful is to rehouse the affected snake in a small cage made to resemble its natural environment. The container should be maintained in total darkness, heated to at least 80° F, and screened on all sides to minimize disturbance. Food items should be offered at intervals of several days although they may not be accepted for some weeks. When the snake has regained its confidence and is feeding regularly it is best transferred to a more hygienic arrangement.

This procedure should be postponed in the case of a weak or emaciated snake. Tube-feeding should instead be implemented until the patient is sufficiently fit to undergo the aforementioned treatment. Initially it would be wise to attempt tube-feeding only under professional supervision as it requires a certain amount of practical experience. The technique involves forcing a liquified food medium into the stomach by means of a narrow lubricated tube and syringe that, needless to say, should be sterilized before and after use. The mixture should be of a fairly thick consistency as it can be unintentionally regurgitated if too dilute. A combination of minced heart and liver appears to be the most versatile tubing food; vitamin preparations and medications can be added if required. Long-term use of this technique should be avoided as it may considerably delay the transition to voluntary feeding.

Force-feeding solid food is rather more difficult. Unless it is performed with the greatest of care, the snake may suffer from stress or even injury, in which case the food is almost always rejected.

It is often a frustrating task to induce those snakes that naturally feed upon difficult to obtain animals, such as other reptiles, to accept an item of food more readily available. This often can be overcome by transferring the scent of preferred food onto a more practical food, or vice versa. For example, a strip of meat can be wrapped in a cast snake skin to entice ophiophagus species or a dead mouse smothered with the scent of a lizard to persuade lizard-eating species to feed. In this way a snake can often be weaned onto food that would normally be quite unacceptable.

HANDLING

Generally speaking, the same rules can be applied to handling pythons and boas as to most other nonvenomous snakes. The larger species, however, obviously need additional support and the keeper may require assistance, especially if those he intends to handle are unpredictable or aggressive.

Many species of boids can be handled freely without attempting to bite, yet others are virtually impossible to subdue. Tree boas *(Corallus)*, particularly wild-caught adults, are by most accounts very aggressive and can inflict a painful bite. These and similar species can be restrained with a standard snakestick or grasped behind the head with the thumb and forefinger or pilstrom tongs. Heavy-bodied snakes should never be pinned to the floor with a stick as most will undoubtedly resort to violent struggles that cause unnecessary stress and can result in serious injury. Instead they should be lifted at mid-body with a snakestick or preferably by hand, always taking care to distribute the weight equally.

Snakes will occasionally regurgitate food if for some reason they do not feel at ease, so they should not be handled before a meal is offered or immediately after it is consumed.

Some species resort to the distasteful habit of defecating or releasing musk when handled. A recipient of this odorous attention may find the experience alarming to say the least, but it is only a natural reaction to fear that will cease, temper permitting, if the culprit is handled regularly.

The keeper who seriously intends to breed his snakes would be ill-advised to handle them during the breeding season. Some enthusiasts maintain that handling does not interfere with precopulatory habits, but especially in the case of nervous and easily discouraged varieties it may prove advantageous not to do so in the long run.

All snakes should be handled cautiously, as even the most trustworthy can at times be unpredictable. They should not be held close to the face or abused in any way. Two or more handlers may be necessary to safely handle a very large python or boa. Skilled handlers are invariably those who respect their animals regardless of how large or small, dangerous or placid they may be.

Temperament of pythons and boas varies considerably both within and among the species. Some species, such as the green tree boa (above), are almost always vicious, striking savagely even after months in captivity. Others, such as the Burmese rock python (below), rapidly adjust to captivity and usually make docile pets, but even they can have their bad moments—and if the snake is 10 or 15 feet long, very bad moments indeed. Photos by K. Lucas at Steinhart Aquarium.

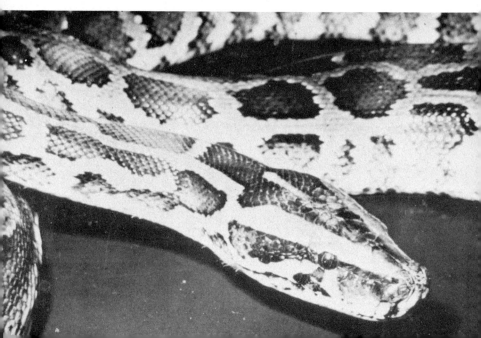

PARASITES AND DISEASES

This section endeavors to discuss only those ailments that, within certain limits, the keeper can himself diagnose and treat. At present there are no legal quarantine requirements for reptiles or amphibians entering the commercial market in the U.S.A. or Great Britain. The keeper therefore becomes directly responsible for the health of his new acquisition and is advised to take precautions against possible spread of disease throughout his established collection. He should also, for that matter, become acquainted with symptoms related to diseases that may endanger his own health. Of potential harm to the keeper are certain bacterial infections such as those caused by *Salmonella* and also a few internal parasites, both of which are discussed later.

A suspiciously ill or recently acquired snake should be isolated and housed in a small, easily cleaned vivarium that is disinfected before and after use. This should be heated to the patient's optimum temperature range (usually about 85° F) and should contain only a hiding box and a water bowl. Snakes harboring a disease are likely to develop clinical symptoms during the period of isolation and can be treated accordingly. Two weeks is the minimum quarantine recommended. This is considered sufficient time for any trace of a dormant disease to become apparent, but it should be extended if an illness is suspected. Additions to the collection should be inspected on arrival and at regular intervals throughout this period. It would also be wise to submit any fatalities to an animal pathologist for postmorten examination, as the information obtained would undoubtedly be of future use to the keeper.

Whenever possible, a qualified veterinarian should be consulted before attempting to treat an ailing reptile. Professional help is invaluable but sometimes hard to find, for the average practicing vet is often at a loss for what to do when confronted with such an unfamiliar creature. Fortunately, specific information regarding diagnosis and treatment is not so scant as it once was and there are now several reliable publications available to which the bewildered enthusiast can refer.

Mites and Ticks

Many wild-caught snakes harbor a variety of both external and internal parasites. Ticks and mites congregate under the scales and around the eyes. Large infestations can cause anemia or transmit disease and should be eradicated as quickly as possible. This was at one time a very difficult problem to overcome, but an effective solution has now been provided in the form of a plastic block or strip impregnated with insecticide (marketed under various names, such as Vapona and No-Pest). This should be left in the affected snake's vivarium for a few hours each day for about a week and replaced for a similar duration a few days later to deal with any larvae that may have hatched in the meantime. Extreme caution should be exercised when using this product in confined spaces as continual overexposure can easily endanger the health of the snake.

Mites in particular can soon reach epidemic proportions, in which event it is best to restrain the patient in a shallow bath of warm water for several hours. This will effectively drown the majority of mites, but the insecticide strip treatment should also be applied to make perfectly sure. Ticks are often large enough to remove individually. A dab of petroleum jelly is first placed on the tick, making it loosen its hold. It can then be slowly withdrawn taking care not to leave the mouthparts behind, which could cause infection.

Worms

Internal parasites such as roundworms (Nematoda), tapeworms (Cestoda), and flukes (Trematoda) present a

Large boas and pythons sometimes arrive absolutely covered with ticks, as is this rainbow boa. Such heavy infestations may lead to trouble with feeding and shedding of the skin as well as possibly anemia. Photos by G. Marcuse.

different problem. Although many species are harmless, they can reduce the overall condition of the affected animal by living off ingested food and blood and should be eliminated to avoid problems of a secondary nature.

Pythons and boas are particularly vulnerable to ascarid nematode infestations. In large numbers these worms can cause blockages in the alimentary canal and lead to troublesome infections such as inflammation of the stomach wall. Typical symptoms include a ravenous appetite coupled with an inability to put on any significant weight. These helminths vary from a fraction of an inch to several inches in length and are cylindrical in shape. Adult and larval stages can be found in virtually every organ of the body. Mature nematodes are sometimes regurgitated but are more often passed through with fecal matter. Many pet-worming tablets containing piperazine will effectively remove ascarid nematodes, though piperazine must be used with great caution and the dosage carefully adjusted to body weight.

The boids frequently act as hosts to tapeworms, sometimes supporting large numbers in the intestine. Adult tapeworms are clearly segmented and ribbon-like in appearance, occasionally reaching astonishing lengths. Specimens in excess of 15 feet have been recorded! Individual segments filled with eggs are regularly passed through with fecal matter. The larval stages eventually become encysted in various parts of the host and are recognizable in some cases as small blisters just under the skin. Symptoms of heavy tapeworm infestations include a ravenous appetite or complete loss of appetite and anemia. Specific worming preparations can

Smears of the fecal matter of snakes will often reveal the eggs of parasitic worms. In fishes and mammals the eggs are well known and can be used to identify the worms before initiating the precise treatment, but in snakes the parasites are less thoroughly known. Shown are rather typical eggs of trematodes or flukes (numbers 1 to 5), cestodes or tapeworms (6 to 9), acanthocephalans or thorny-headed worms (10 to 15), and nematodes (16 to 21). After Reichenbach-Klinke.

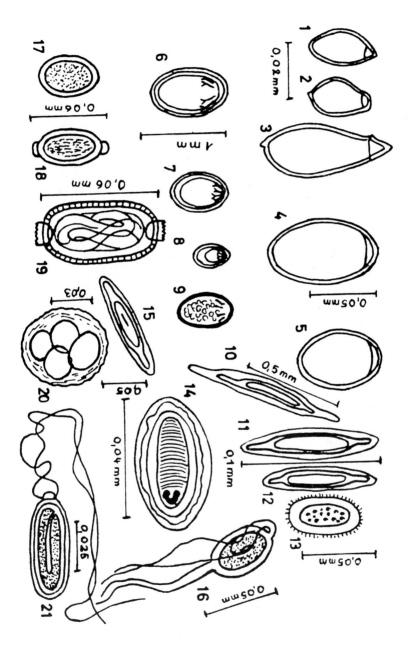

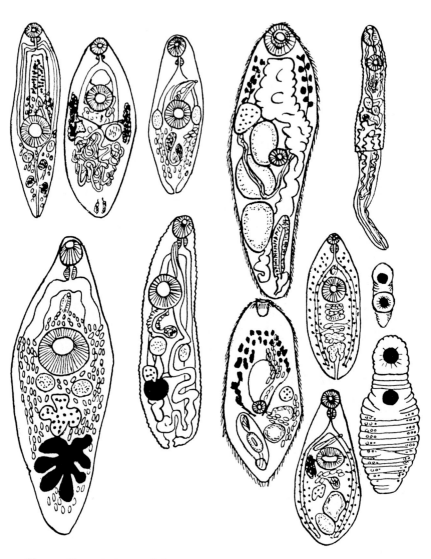

Above: Trematodes or flukes occur in a bewildering array of shapes and sizes, but those likely to be found in the gut of snakes will look at least similar to the ones shown here. Notice the presence of two sucking discs on the body, typical of intestinal flukes. After Reichenbach-Klinke.

Facing page: Diagram of the life cycle of a typical fluke. The metacercariae are often ingested by snakes that eat fishes and birds, main hosts of many flukes. If the metacercariae fail to develop in the snake's intestines, they will sometimes encyst below the skin and be visible as small black nodules. After Reichenbach-Klinke.

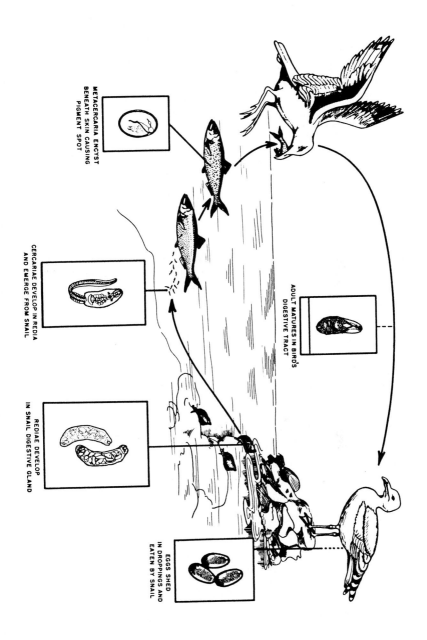

METACERCARIA ENCYST
BENEATH SKIN CAUSING
PIGMENT SPOT

CERCARIAE DEVELOP IN REDIA
AND EMERGE FROM SNAIL

ADULT MATURES IN BIRD'S
DIGESTIVE TRACT

REDIAE DEVELOP
IN SNAIL DIGESTIVE GLAND

EGGS SHED
IN DROPPINGS AND
EATEN BY SNAIL

153

The "heads" or proboscises of acanthocephalans or thorny-headed worms. These parasites are often very common in the intestines of snakes, boids included, but don't seem to cause a great deal of damage.

be obtained from veterinarians, but care must be taken to administer the correct dosage in relation to body weight, as with any worming medication.

These two groups of internal parasites are relatively easy to treat as they are susceptible to orally-administered anthelminthics that reach the digestive tract. Those worms that infest the respiratory and circulatory systems are, however, not so accessible. Digenetic flukes fall into this category, although they are not considered a serious threat in comparison to nematodes and cestodes. Lungworms have also been found to infest pythons and boas. As the common name suggests, they are located in the trachea and bronchial tracts. Affected snakes have difficulty in breathing, often holding the mouth slightly agape. Accompanying symptoms include a loss of appetite and a distended throat region. First-stage larvae can be found on microscopic examination of oral mucus or fecal matter.

Positive treatment of any internal parasite can only be effected by determining the species involved. It would be pointless listing possible remedies for treating each individual group as not only are they extremely numerous, but very few respond to the same specific drugs.

Gastroenteritis

Pythons and boas occasionally fall victim to a serious form of parasitic disease similar to gastroenteritis in mammals. This is caused by protozoans of the genus *Entamoeba*. These single-celled organisms attack the mucous membrane of the intestine and its capillary structure, spreading throughout the host via the bloodstream. Affected areas usually suffer severe damage and invariably become infected. The feces of contaminated snakes are sometimes of a mushy consistency and pale in color. They may reveal encysted amoebal parasites on microscopic examination. Snakes suffering from this disease drink regularly, are lethargic, and refuse to feed. Death can occur within a matter of days unless immediate steps are taken to counteract the disease. There are several courses of treatment, the most reliable involving the use of antiprotozoal drugs such as iodochlorhydroxyquinoline (Vioform).

Bacterial Infections

The most commonly encountered form of bacterial infection in snakes is mouth rot or ulcerative stomatitis, which is usually caused by members of the genera *Pseudomonas* and *Aeromonas*. This disease usually occurs in stressed, undernourished reptiles and those that have been neglected. Symptoms include loss of appetite, a pale or discolored mouth lining, hemorrhaging gums, and patches of decaying tissue producing cheesey deposits within the mouth. The accepted treatment consists of thoroughly irrigating the mouth cavity with an antiseptic solution such as dilute hydrogen peroxide and a broad-spectrum antibiotic. Vitamin supplements, particularly those preparations containing A and C, are also recommended by many authorities.

These bacteria are also responsible for a similar disease affecting the skin. This condition is typically characterized by the appearance of numerous small blisters, shrivelled head shields, and discolored ventral scales. In severe examples the tissue under the lower jaw disintegrates, sometimes exposing the bones. This disease develops rapidly and, unless caught at an early stage, will almost certainly lead to the reptile's death. An antibiotic can be administered by means of a stomach catheter or injected intramuscularly. Areas of skin deterioration should be bathed with warm water daily and treated with an iodine-based antiseptic.

The variety of bacteria to be found in the gastrointestinal tract comprise a list far too long to enumerate. Most are not only harmless but actually play an essential role in the digestion of food, so it would be pointless to remove them. The genus of bacteria known as *Salmonella*, however, is worthy of attention as it can be transmitted to humans with serious consequences. Infected snakes can carry the disease (called salmonella poisoning or salmonellosis) without any apparent discomfort but may suffer from internal problems. In humans the disease is usually a mild type of food-poisoning. Salmonellosis in reptiles can be treated with antibiotics, but the only visible indication of its presence may be a change in behavior or loss of appetite. A fecal sample should be submitted for examination if the keeper becomes suspicious.

Nutritional Diseases
The boids will avoid most forms of nutritional disease

if fed correctly on whole food items. Calcium and vitamin deficiencies are probably the only afflictions a keeper will encounter, and these for the most part are usually confined to very young snakes. Lack of calcium, although affecting many other bodily functions, leads primarily to abnormal bone development by depleting vital reserves in the skeleton, but it may also be a cause of constipation and paralysis. It is a good idea to occasionally give captive boids ground cuttlefish bone either sprinkled over food or dissolved in drinking water to be sure of providing sufficient calcium. Vitamin deficiencies are probably the most difficult to diagnose as they can manifest themselves in any number of ways. For this reason it may be advisable to add a few drops of a multivitamin preparation to the food of very young snakes. The moral "prevention is better than cure" should be applied here, for many complaints caused by vitamin and calcium deficiencies are generally irreversible. It may also be worth noting that overweight snakes tend to be sexually impotent and less resistant to disease.

Colds

Colds are a particularly common occurrence among snakes, and if left untreated they can prove fatal. Affected animals can be easily recognized. The mouth is choked with excessive mucous secretions and is held slightly agape when normal breathing through the nostrils becomes impossible. Colds are usually caused by subjecting the animal to drafts or long periods at low temperatures. Mild cases can often be successfully cured by simply raising the temperataure of the vivarium to about 90° F and supplementing the diet with vitamin C in the form of ascorbic acid tablets. Serious attacks call for more positive measures such as the use of antibiotics. The drug chloromycetin has been used successfully to cure reptilian colds.

Peritonitis

Peritonitis is a very serious condition of the digestive tract that unfortunately rarely becomes apparent until the affected snake is close to death. It is usually caused by the ingestion of an abrasive particle or too large a meal that scratches or ruptures the intestinal wall. The damaged area becomes acutely infected and swells, preventing food from progressing any further. The meal then decomposes without being digested, causing the intestine to "bloat" out of all proportion. To reduce the risk of peritonitis the keeper should avoid using sand as a substrate or should feed the snake in a separate container.

9: Informal Key to the Boid Genera

The following key is presented strictly as an aid in placing specimens in the correct genus or generic group. It is not intended to be exhaustive in its characterization and may not work for all species, especially in the confusing *Python* - *Liasis* group. For more comprehensive definitions and keys to the genera see McDowell, 1975 and 1979. *Xenoboa* and *Exiliboa* are not keyed. *Xenoboa* would probably key out to *Epicrates*, though with 36 or fewer scale rows versus over 40 in *Epicrates*, but it is at best poorly known. *Exiliboa* is somewhat similar to *Ungaliophis* in scalation but has a virtually all-black body color and undivided nasal scales with a single internasal.

1a. Subcaudal scales usually in two rows (except *Aspidites*); supraorbital bone present 2
1b. Subcaudal scales usually in a single row; supraorbital bone absent 7
2a. Premaxilla with teeth 3
2b. Premaxilla without teeth 5
3a. Anterior supralabials and rostral scale with deep pits; tail may be prehensile .... *Python*
3b. Rostral scale without pits or with only shallow pits; tail usually not prehensile 4
4a. No pits no supralabials; New World .... *Loxocemus*
4b. Pits present on supralabials; Australasia .... *Liasis*
5a. Tail tapered to a point, obviously different from head; palatine teeth present 6
5b. Tail very short, blunt, similar to head in shape; palatine teeth absent .... *Calabaria*
6a. Labials with deep, conspicuous pits; subcaudals in two rows .... *Chondropython*
6b. Labials without apparent pits; subcaudals mostly in one row .... *Aspidites*
7a. Head continuing smoothly into body, no obvious neck; tail not prehensile 8
7b. Head separated from body by distinct neck; tail usually somewhat prehensile 11
8a. Most midbody scales with more than two keels (ridges); Round Island .... *Bolyeria*

159

8b. Midbody scales smooth or with a single keel 9
9a. Shields on top of head fragmented into many small scales
.... 10
9b. Shields on top of head large, regular in shape and placement .... *Charina*
10a. Rostral scale usually very large; color pattern usually banded, blotched, or plain, not striped; Old World .....
.... *Eryx*
10b. Rostral scale distinctly higher than wide, but of relatively moderate size; color pattern of three dark stripes; New World .... *Lichanura*
11a. Anterior teeth much enlarged 12
11b. Teeth regularly decreasing in size from anterior to posterior in upper jaw, the anterior teeth not markedly larger than the middle teeth 14
12a. Scales keeled; Pacific islands .... *Candoia*
12b. Scales smooth; New World and Madagascar 13
13a. Labials with shallow or inconspicuous pits ..... *Epicrates*
13b. Labials with deep, distinct pits ....
.... *Corallus* (New World) + *Sanzinia* (Madagascar)
14a. Scales keeled 15
14b. Scales smooth or nearly so 16
15a. Keels moderately heavy; Round Island .... *Casarea*
15b. Keels extremely strong, even on head, often erect at the tip to produce upright spines on head and lower sides of body; New World .... *Trachyboa*
16a. Scales small, crowded, more than 40 at midbody
.... 17
16b. Scales larger, colubrid in appearance, fewer than 30 at midbody 18
17a. Nostrils distinctly dorsal; nasal shields in contact behind rostral shield .... *Eunectes*
17b. Nostrils lateral or dorsolateral; nasal shields separated by small scales ....
.... *Boa* (New World) + *Acrantophis* (Madagascar)
18a. Prefrontals in one or two pairs; color pattern simple, of spots, blotches, or bars .... *Tropidophis*
18b. Prefrontal single, exceptionally large; color pattern complex .... *Ungaliophis*

10: A Checklist of Pythons and Boas

The following checklist, condensed in part from "Liste der rezenten Amphibien und Reptilien, Boidae" (Stimson, 1969), is presented chiefly as a convenient listing of pythons and boas, but an attempt has also been made to bring the classification of these snakes more into line with modern herpetological views. The taxonomic arrangement of some species, however, especially those within the subfamily Pythoninae, remains open to dispute. I have in general followed McDowell (1975) in his treatment of this critical group, but consideration of the Pythoninae would be incomplete without reference to Cogger, Cameron, and Cogger (1983), in whose account of Australian species the generic name *Liasis* is replaced by *Bothrochilus (Liasis* itself becomes a synonym of *Morelia)*, and the genus *Morelia* is resurrected to include all other Australian pythons except *Chondropython* and *Aspidites*. Another recent interpretation of the relationships of pythons in this part of the world, if somewhat inconsistent with others, is given by Wells and Wellington (1983).

Distributions are as detailed as space will allow, but where taxa occur sporadically over extensive island ranges (e.g., *Candoia* in the SW Pacific and *Epicrates* in the Caribbean) only the main island groups are listed. Also, it may not necessarily follow that species occupy

Epicrates inornatus, the Puerto Rican boa. The juvenile pattern is shown above. Photos by Phillip Coffey, J. W. P. T.

Epicrates angulifer, the Cuban boa. Photo by Phillip Coffey, J. W. P. T.

the total area of a country listed. Where a country represents the outer limits of distribution, for example, the species concerned may only be of peripheral occurrence. For more detailed accounts of distribution the selection of literature provided in the bibliography should be consulted.

A taxon thought to be of uncertain status is denoted by a star (★). Those synonyms that are still in frequent use can be found listed in parentheses after the appropriate name.

Subfamily Boinae

Genus *Acrantophis* Jan, 1860

A. *dumerili*	Jan, 1860	Madagascar and Reunion.
A. *madagascariensis*	(Dumeril & Bibron, 1844)	Madagascar.

Genus *Boa* Linnaeus, 1758 (*Constrictor*)

B. *constrictor*:

constrictor constrictor	Linnaeus, 1758	N South America from Venezuela to Bolivia and S Brazil; Trinidad and Tobago.
constrictor amarali	(Stull, 1932)	E Bolivia; N and C Brazil.
constrictor imperator	Daudin, 1803	C and N South America from S Mexico to NW Peru.
constrictor melanogaster	Langhammer, 1983	Ecuador.
constrictor nebulosa	(Lazell, 1964)	Dominica, Lesser Antilles.
constrictor occidentalis	Philippi, 1873	Argentina and Paraguay.
constrictor orophias	Linnaeus, 1758	St. Lucia, Lesser Antilles.
★constrictor sigma	(Smith, 1943)	Tres Marias Is., Mexico.

Genus *Candoia* Gray, 1842 (*Enygrus*)

C. *aspera*	(Gunther, 1877)	New Guinea and adjacent is.; Bismarck Archipelago; Solomon Islands.

C. bibroni:

bibroni bibroni	(Dumeril & Bibron, 1844)	Fiji Is.; Loyalty Is.; Banks Is.; Tonga; Society Is., SW Pacific.
bibroni australis	(Montrouzier, 1860)	Bismarck Archipelago; Solomon Is.; Santa Cruz Is.; New Hebrides; Loyalty Is.; Tokelau Is.; Samoa, SW Pacific.

C. carinata:

carinata carinata	(Schneider, 1801)	Palau Is.; Sulawesi; Moluccas; New Guinea and adjacent is.; Bismarck Archipelago; Tokelau Is., SW Pacific.
carinata paulsoni	(Stull, 1956)	Solomon Is.; Santa Cruz Is., SW Pacific.

Genus *Corallus* Daudin, 1803 (*Boa*)

C. annulatus:

annulatus annulatus	(Cope, 1876)	S Nicaragua to NW Colombia.
★*annulatus blombergi*	(Rendahl & Vestergren, 1941)	E Ecuador.
annulatus colombianus	(Rendahl & Vestergren, 1940)	SW Colombia; NW Ecuador.
C. caninus	(Linnaeus, 1758)	Amazon Basin from Venezuela through Brazil to N Bolivia.

C. *enydris*:

enydris enydris	(Linnaeus, 1758)	N, E and C South America.
enydris cookii (*Boa cooki*)	Gray, 1842	C and NW South America from Nicaragua to Peru; Trinidad and Windward Is.

Genus *Epicrates* Wagler, 1830

E. *angulifer*	Cocteau & Bibron, 1840	Cuba and satellite is.

E. *cenchria*:

cenchria cenchria	(Linnaeus, 1758)	Amazon Basin; Venezuela and Guianas.
cenchria alvarezi	Abalos, Baez & Nader, 1964	NC Argentina.
★*cenchria assisi*	Machado, 1944	Piaui and Bahia, NW Brazil.
cenchria barbouri	Stull, 1938	Para, N Brazil.
cenchria crassus	Cope, 1862	S and C Brazil; Paraguay; NE Argentina.
cenchria gaigei	Stull, 1938	Bolivia, C and S Peru.
cenchria hygrophilus	Amaral, 1954	Amazonas and Espirito Santo, Brazil.
cenchria maurus	Gray, 1849	Costa Rica S to Venezuela, Colombia, and the Guianas.
cenchria polylepis	Amaral, 1935	E Brazil.

Taxon	Authority	Distribution
cenchria xerophilus	Amaral, 1954	NE Brazil.
E. chrysogaster:		
chrysogaster chrysogaster	(Cope, 1871)	Caicos Is., Bahamas.
chrysogaster relicquus	Barbour & Shreve, 1935	Great Inagua Is., Bahamas.
chrysogaster schwartzi	Buden, 1975	Acklins Is. and Crooked Is., Bahamas.
E. exsul	Netting & Goin, 1944	Abaco Is., Bahamas.
E. fordii:		
fordii fordii	(Gunther, 1861)	Hispaniola.
*fordii agametus	Sheplan & Schwartz, 1974	Haiti.
E. gracilis:		
gracilis gracilis	(Fischer, 1888)	Hispaniola.
gracilis hapalus	Sheplan & Schwartz, 1974	Hispaniola.
E. inornatus	(Reinhardt, 1843)	Puerto Rico.
E. monensis:		
monensis monensis	Zenneck, 1898	Isla Mona, W. Indies.
monensis granti	Stull, 1933	Virgin Is., W. Indies.
E. striatus:		
striatus striatus	(Fischer, 1856)	Hispaniola.
striatus ailurus	Sheplan & Schwartz, 1974	Cat I., Bahamas.

striatus exagistus	Sheplan & Schwartz, 1974	Hispaniola.
striatus fosteri	Barbour, 1941	Bimini Is. and Easter Cay, Bahamas.
striatus fowleri	Sheplan & Schwartz, 1974	Andros I. and Berry Is., Bahamas.
striatus mccraniei	Sheplan & Schwartz, 1974	Ragged Is., Bahamas.
striatus strigilatus	(Cope, 1862)	C Bahamas.
striatus warreni	Sheplan & Schwartz, 1974	Ile de la Tortue, Haiti.
E. subflavus	Stejneger, 1901	Jamaica.

Genus *Eunectes* ·Wagler, 1830

★*E. barbouri*	Dunn & Conant, 1936	Para, Brazil.
★*E. deschauenseei*	Dunn & Conant, 1936	French Guiana; Para State, Brazil.

E. murinus:

murinus murinus (murinus gigas)	(Linnaeus, 1758)	N South America.
murinus scytale (murinus murinus)	(Linnaeus, 1758)	Amazon Basin of Brazil and NW South America.
E. notaeus	Cope, 1862	W and C South America, from S Brazil and Bolivia to Uruguay.

Above: *Epicrates subflavus,* the Jamaican boa. Photo by Phillip Coffey, J. W. P. T. **Below:** *Casarea dussumieri,* one of the Round Island boas. Photo by Phillip Coffey,J. W. P. T.

Genus **Sanzinia** Gray, 1849		
S. madagascariensis	(Dumeril & Bibron, 1844)	Madagascar.
Genus **Xenoboa** Hoge, 1953		
X. cropanii	Hoge, 1953	Sao Paulo State, Brazil.
Subfamily Bolyeriinae		
Genus **Bolyeria** Gray, 1842		
B. multocarinata	(Boie, 1827)	Round I., near Mauritius.
Genus **Casarea** Gray, 1842		
C. dussumieri	(Schlegel, 1837)	Round I., near Mauritius.
Subfamily Calabariinae		
Genus **Calabaria** Gray, 1858		
C. reinhardtii	(Schlegel, 1851)	W. Africa, from Liberia to Gabon and the Congo.
Subfamily Erycinae		
Genus **Charina** Gray, 1849		
C. bottae:		
bottae bottae	(Blainville, 1835)	W coast of North America, from S British Columbia to N California.
★bottae umbratica	Klauber, 1943	S California.
★bottae utahensis	van Denburgh, 1920	W North America from S British Columbia to N Utah.

Genus **Eryx** Daudin, 1803

E. colubrinus: (Eryx thebaicus)

colubrinus colubrinus	(Linnaeus, 1758)	Yemen; NE Africa.
colubrinus loveridgei	Stull, 1932	E. Africa from S Somalia to N Tanzania.

E. conicus: (Gongylophis conicus)

conicus conicus	(Schneider, 1801)	W Pakistan and India.
conicus brevis	Deraniyagala, 1951	Sri Lanka.
E. elegans	(Gray, 1849)	C Asia Minor, from Turkmenistan to NW India.

E. jaculus:

jaculus jaculus	(Linnaeus, 1758)	N Africa from Egypt to Morocco; E to Iran.
jaculus familiaris	Eichwald, 1831	From NW Iraq to E Asia Minor.
jaculus turcicus	(Oliver, 1801)	SE Europe, from Yugoslavia to W Asia Minor.
E. jayakari	Boulenger, 1888	Arabia and SW Asia Minor.

E. johnii:

johnii johnii	(Russell, 1801)	W Pakistan and India.
johnii persicus	Nikolsky, 1907	Asia Minor, from Iraq to N India.

E. miliaris (Pallas, 1773) — C Asia Minor and S U.S.S.R., from Turkmenistan E to W Mongolia.

E. muelleri:
muelleri muelleri (Boulenger, 1892) — W and C Africa.
muelleri subniger Angel, 1938 — NW Africa E to Mali.
E. somalicus Scortecci, 1939 — Somalia.
E. tataricus
tataricus tataricus (Lichtenstein, 1823) — W Asia Minor.
tataricus speciosus Carevsky, 1916 — Tadzhikistan, U.S.S.R.
tataricus vittatus Chernov, 1959 — Asia Minor, from E Iran to W China.

Genus *Lichanura* Cope, 1861
L. trivirgata:
trivirgata trivirgata Cope, 1861 — S Arizona to Mexican border.
trivirgata gracia Klauber, 1931 — SC California to C Arizona.
trivirgata roseofusca Cope, 1868 — S California to Baja Mexico.

Subfamily Loxoceminae
Genus *Loxocemus* Cope, 1861
L. bicolor Cope, 1861 — C America from S Mexico to N Costa Rica.

Subfamily Pythoninae
Genus *Aspidites* Peters, 1876

A. *melanocephalus*	(Krefft, 1864)	N Australia.
A. *ramsayi*	(Macleay, 1882)	SW, C and E Australia.

Genus *Chondropython* Meyer, 1875

C. *viridis*	(Schlegel, 1872)	New Guinea and adjacent Is.; Aru Is.; Cape York Peninsula, Australia.

Genus *Liasis* Gray, 1842

L. *albertisii*	Peters & Doria, 1878	New Guinea; Bismarck Archipelago.
L. *boa* (*Bothrochilus boa*)	(Schlege, 1837)	Bismarck Archipelago.
L. *childreni*	Gray, 1842	Australia excluding far SE.
L. *mackloti* (*L. fuscus*): mackloti mackloti (*L. m. dunni*)	Duméril & Bibron, 1844	New Guinea; N Australia; Lesser Sunda Is., Indonesia.
mackloti savuensis	Brongersma, 1956	Savu I., Indonesia.
L. *olivaceus*: olivaceus olivaceus	Gray, 1842	N. Australia.
olivaceus barroni	(Smith, 1981)	Pilbara region, W. Australia.
L. *papuanus* (*L. maximum*)	Peters & Doria, 1878	New Guinea.

173

Above: *Aspidites melanocephalus,* the black-headed python. Photo by H. G. Cogger. **Below:** *Liasis childreni,* Children's python. Photo by H. G. Cogger.

L. perthensis	Stull, 1932	W. Australia.
Genus ***Python*** Daudin, 1803		
P. amethistinus (Liasis a. amethistinus + L. a. kinghorni)	(Schneider, 1801)	Is. of E Indonesia; New Guinea; Bismarck Archipelago.
P. anchietae	Bocage, 1887	S Angola; N South-West Africa.
P. boeleni (Liasis taronga)	Brongersma, 1953	New Guinea.
P. bredli	Gow, 1981	C Australia.
⋆*P. carinatus*	(Smith, 1981)	W Australia.
P. curtus:		
curtus curtus	Schlegel, 1872	W Sumatra.
curtus breitensteini	Steindachner, 1880	Borneo.
curtus brongersmai	Stull, 1938	S Indo-China and E Sumatra.
P. molurus:		
molurus molurus (P. m. pimbura)	(Linnaeus, 1758)	India; W Pakistan to Nepal; Sri Lanka.
molurus bivittatus	Kuhl, 1820	Indo-China; Malaysia and W Indonesia.
P. oenpelliensis	Gow, 1977	W Arnhem Land, Northern Territory, Australia.

P. regius	(Shaw, 1802)	W and C Africa, from Senegal to Uganda.
P. reticulatus	(Schneider, 1801)	Indo-China; Malaysia and Indonesia N to Philippines.
P. sebae:		
sebae sebae	(Gmelin, 1789)	Africa S of Sahara, from Senegal E to Ethiopia and S to Angola.
sebae natalensis (P. saxuloides)	Smith, 1840	C and S Africa, from Kenya S to Angola and NE South Africa.
P. spilotes (Morelia spilotes, M. argus)		
spilotes spilotes	(Lacepede, 1804)	Coast of New South Wales, Australia.
spilotes imbricatus	(Smith, 1981)	SW Australia.
★spilotes macrospila	Werner, 1909	Holotype from unknown locality.
spilotes variegatus	(Gray, 1824)	Australia, from Kimberley region through top of Northern Territory, Queensland, and New South Wales to S South Australia.
P. timorensis	(Peters, 1876)	Timor and Flores, Indonesia

Above: *Python amethistinus*, the amethistine python. Photo by
H. G. Cogger. **Below:** *Python spilotes variegatus*, a carpet python.
Photo by H. G. Cogger.

Subfamily Tropidophiinae
Genus *Exiliboa* Bogert, 1968

Taxon	Author	Distribution
E. placata	Bogert, 1968	Oaxaca, Mexico.
Genus *Trachyboa* Peters, 1860		
T. boulengeri	Peracca, 1910	NW South America, from Panama through Colombia to Ecuador.
T. gularis	Peters, 1860	W Ecuador.
Genus *Tropidophis* Bibron, 1843 (*Ungalia*)		
T. battersbyi	Laurent, 1949	Ecuador.
T. canus:		
canus canus	(Cope, 1868)	Great Inagua I., Bahamas.
canus androsi	Stull, 1927	Andros I., Bahamas.
canus barbouri	Bailey, 1937	Bahama Is.
canus curtus	(Garman, 1887)	Bimini Is. and New Providence I., Bahamas.
T. caymanensis:		
caymanensis caymanensis	Battersby, 1938	Grand Cayman I., Cayman Is.
caymanensis parkeri	Grant, 1941	Little Cayman I., Cayman Is.
caymanensis schwartzi	Thomas, 1963	Cayman Brac I., Cayman Is.
T. feicki	Schwartz, 1957	W. Cuba.

Taxon	Authority	Distribution
T. greenwayi:		
greenwayi greenwayi	Barbour & Shreve, 1936	Ambergis Cay, Caicos Is. (Bahamas).
greenwayi lanthanus	Schwartz, 1963	Caicos Is., Bahamas.
T. haetianus:		
haetianus haetianus	(Cope, 1879)	E. Cuba; Hispaniola.
haetianus hemerus	Schwartz, 1975	Dominican Republic, Hispaniola.
haetianus jamaicensis	Stull, 1928	S Jamaica.
haetianus stejnegeri	Grant, 1940	N Jamaica.
haetianus stullae	Grant, 1940	Portland Point, Jamaica.
haetianus tiburonensis	Schwartz, 1975	Tiburon Peninsula, Haiti.
T. maculatus	(Bibron, 1843)	W Cuba and Isla de Pinos.
T. melanurus:		
melanurus melanurus	(Schlegel, 1837)	Cuba.
melanurus bucculentus	(Cope, 1868)	Navassa I, Haiti.
melanurus dysodes	Schwartz & Thomas, 1960	Pinar del Rio Province, Cuba.
melanurus ericksoni	Schwartz & Thomas, 1960	Isla de Pinos, Cuba.
T. nigriventris:		
nigriventris nigriventris	Bailey, 1937	Camaguey Province, Cuba.

179

nigriventris hardyi	Schwartz & Garrido, 1975	Las Villas Province, Cuba.
T. pardalis	(Gundlach, 1840)	Cuba.
T. paucisquamis	(Mueller, 1901)	SE Brazil and NE Peru.
T. pilsbryi:		
pilsbryi pilsbryi	Bailey, 1937	E Cuba.
pilsbryi galacelidus	Schwartz & Garrido, 1975	Las Villas Province, Cuba.
T. semicinctus	(Gundlach & Peters, 1864)	W and C Cuba.
T. taczanowskyi	(Steindachner, 1880)	Amazonian Peru and Ecuador.
T. wrighti	Stull, 1938	E Cuba.
Genus ***Ungaliophis*** Muller, 1880		
U. continentalis	Muller, 1880	Chiapas, Mexico to Honduras.
U. panamensis	Schmidt, 1933	S Nicaragua to W Colombia.

Appendix: Convention on International Trade in Endangered Species of Wild Fauna and Flora (CITES)

All species of python and boa are listed in the appendices of endangered taxa compiled by CITES, the agreement by which legislation is provided to control the international shipment of animals, plants, and their products between member nations. Those species that are in the most immediate danger of extinction, as listed in the *Red Data Book*, appear as *Appendix 1* entries and receive the strongest protective measures, including the prohibition of commercial trade. A species designated under *Appendix 2* of the Convention requires a special permit to be exported from its country of origin or re-exported if it is held elsewhere, and some countries may also require another permit to authorize importation. Under certain circumstances (*i.e.*, in the case of captive-bred specimens) special permission to export *Appendix 1* or *2* species may be granted in the form of a *Certificate of Exception*. The purpose and function of *Appendix 3* is to enable countries to call on the assistance of other Party States in protecting their native species that although not of *Appendix 1* or *2* status are protected in the country concerned.

It is worth noting that subspecific forms of some taxa may be placed in different appendices according to their individual status of survival. The Indo-Chinese form of the Asiatic rock python *(Python molurus bivittatus)*, for example, is listed in *Appendix 2*, but the rare nominate form *(Python molurus molurus)* from India and Sri Lanka appears under *Appendix 1*. Provided below is a full list of pythons and boas that presently appear in *Appendix 1*. All other boids are classified under *Appendix 2*.

Appendix 1 species

Dumeril's boa	*(Acrantophis dumerili)*
Madagascar boa	*(Acrantophis madagascariensis)*
Round Island boa	*(Bolyeria multocarinata)*
Keel-scaled boa	*(Casarea dussumieri)*
Puerto Rican boa	*(Epicrates inornatus)*
Jamaican boa	*(Epicrates subflavus)*
Asiatic rock python	*(Python molurus molurus)*
Madagascar tree boa	*(Sanzinia madagascariensis)*

In addition to the restrictions imposed by CITES, individual countries may also maintain stricter measures to control the import and export of certain animals and plants, and not necessarily to or from parties to the Convention. Where the United Kingdom and other European Common Market countries are concerned, for example, controls over the import of some boids *(i.e.,* the boa constrictor, *Boa constrictor* ssp., and European sand boa, *Eryx jaculus* ssp.) and all species of python and anaconda go much further than the CITES convention.

Glossary

Arboreal—Tree-dwelling.

Aquatic—Water-inhabiting.

Canopy—Closed screen of top-most branches over the forest-floor.

Cranial—Pertaining to the skull.

Cloaca—Common chamber into which digestive, urinary, and reproductive systems empty.

Crepuscular—Active at dusk and/or dawn.

Cryptic—Camouflaged, concealed.

Diurnal—Active by day.

Dorsal—Pertaining to the upper surface.

Ecology—The study of organisms in relation to their environment.

Ectothermic—Cold-blooded; dependent on external source of heat.

Endemic—Found only in one (usually small) geographic area.

Epidermal.—Pertaining to the skin.

Estivation.—Dormancy during the summer or dry season.

Fossorial.—Adapted to burrowing.

Habitat.—Natural residence of an organism.

Helminth.—A parasitic worm inhabiting the digestive, respiratory, or circulatory system of an animal.

Hemipene.—One of the paired sexual organs of male snakes and lizards.

Herpetology.—The study of reptiles and amphibians.

Hibernation.—Dormancy during the winter or cool season.

Keeled.—Ridged; usually applies to dorsal scales.

Keratin.—The dead, horny, relatively inflexible skin of which scales are made.

Labial.—Pertaining to the scales bordering the mouth of lizards and snakes.

Mimicry.—One animal imitating the coloration and/or actions of another.

Monitor.—A lizard of the family Varanidae.

Monotypic Genus.—Genus possessing a single species.

Morphology.—The study of the structure of plants and animals.

New World.—The Americas.

Nocturnal.—Active by night.

Old World.—Continents of Europe, Asia, Africa, and Australia.

Ophiophagus.—An animal that feeds predominantly on snakes.

Oviparous.—An animal that lay eggs.

Parallelism.—Development of two similar species from different ancestors.

Parasite.—An organism deriving its nourishment from another.

Pelvic spurs.—Visible remnants of the hind legs located either side of the vent in boids and a few other snakes.

Prehensile.—Capable of grasping.

Rostral.—Scale at tip of snout.

Spermatogenesis.—Development of sperm.

Subcaudals.—Scales on the ventral surface between the vent and tip of the tail.

Subterranean.—An existence beneath the ground.

Sympatric.—Animals that coexist in the same region.

Taxonomy.—The science of classifying organisms.

Terrestrial.—Ground-dwelling.

Ventral.—Pertaining to the lower surface.

Vivarium.—Container or enclosure for housing reptiles and amphibians.

Viviparous.—Live-bearing.

Xeric.—Hot and dry conditions.

Bibliography

Barnett, B. 1980. "Captive breeding and a novel egg incubation technique of the Children's python (*Liasis childreni*)," *Herpetofauna*, 11(2):15-18.

Bellairs, A. d'A. 1969. *The Life of Reptiles*. 2 vols. Weidenfeld & Nicolson, London.

Bogert, C. M. 1968. "A new genus and species of dwarf boa from southern Mexico," *Amer. Mus. Novitates*.

Bogert, C. M. 1968. "The variations and affinities of the dwarf boas of the genus *Ungaliophis*," *Amer. Mus. Novitates*.

Boulenger, G. A. 1893. *Catalogue of the Snakes in the British Museum*. British Museum (Natural History), London.

Broadley, D. G. 1984. "A review of geographical variation in the African python, *Python sebae* (Gmelin)," *British J. Herpet.*, 6(10): 359-367.

Cogger, H. G. 1979. *Reptiles and Amphibians of Australia*. A. H. & A. W. Reed, Sydney.

Cogger, H. G., E. E. Cameron & H. M. Cogger. 1983. *Zoological Catalogue of Australia. Vol. 1. Amphibia and Reptiles*. Australian Govt. Publ. Serv., Canberra.

Coote, J. 1978. "Feeding captive snakes," *Herptile*, 3(1): 13-17.

Dixon, J. R. & P. Soini. 1977. "Reptiles of the Upper Amazon Basin, Iquitos region, Peru," *Contrib. Biol. & Geol.*, Milwaukee Public Museum, Milwaukee, Wisc.

FitzSimons, V. F. M. 1930. *Pythons and Their Ways*. Harrap, London.

Frank, W. 1979. *Boas and Other Non-venomous Snakes*. T.F.H. Publ., Neptune, NJ.

Frieberg, M. 1982. *Snakes of South America*. T.F.H. Publ., Neptune, NJ.

Frye, F. L. 1981. *Biomedical and Surgical Aspects of*

Captive Reptile Husbandry. V. M. Publications, Edwardsville, Kansas.

Gow, G. F. 1983. *Snakes of Australia.* Angus & Robertson, Australia.

Granger, A. M. 1982. "Notes on the captive breeding of the desert rosy boa *(Lichanura trivirgata gracia),*" *Herptile,* 7(3): 5-7.

Groombridge, B. 1983. *World Checklist of Endangered Amphibians and Reptiles.* Nature Conservancy Council, London.

Grzimek, B. 1975. *Animal Life Encyclopedia. Vol. 16. Reptiles.* Van Nostrand Reinhold Co., New York.

Hay, M. 1971. "Notes on breeding and growth rate of *Morelia spilotes spilotes,*" *Herpetofauna,* 3: 10.

International Union for Conservation of Nature (IUCN). 1979. *Red Data Book 3. Amphibians and Reptiles.* 3rd Ed. Compiled by R. E. Honegger. Morges, Switzerland.

Langhammer, J. K. 1983. "A new subspecies of boa constrictor, *Boa constrictor melanogaster,* from Ecuador," *Tropical Fish Hobbyist,* 32(4): 70-79.

Laszlo, J. 1975. "Probing as a practical method of sex recognition in snakes," *Int. Zoo Yearbook,* 15: 178.

Logan, T. 1973. "Observations on the ball python *(Python regius)* in captivity at Houston Zoological Gardens," *J. Herp. Assoc. Afr.,* #10: 5-8.

Logan, T. 1973. "A note on attempted breeding in captive *Python anchietae,*" *J. Herp. Assoc. Afr.,* #10: 8.

Loveridge, A. (1974). *Reptiles of the Pacific World.* Facsimile Reprints in Herpet., Soc. Study Amphibians and Reptiles, Ohio.

Marcus, L. C. 1981. *Veterinary Biology and Medicine of Captive Amphibians and Reptiles.* Lea & Febiger, Philadelphia.

McCoy, M. 1980. *Reptiles of the Solomon Islands.* Wau Ecology Inst. Handbook #7.

McDowell, S. B. 1975. "A catalogue of the snakes of New Guinea and the Solomons, with special reference to those in the Bernice P. Bishop Museum. Part 2. Anilioidae and Pythoninae," *J. Herpet.*, 9(1): 1-79.

McDowell, S. B. 1979. "A catalogue of the snakes of New Guinea and the Solomons, with special reference to those in the Bernice P. Bishop Museum. Part 3. Boinae and Acrochordoidea," *J. Herpet.*, 13(1): 1-92.

Noble, G. K. 1935. "The breeding habits of the blood python and of other snakes," *Copeia*, 1935(1): 1-3.

Parker, H. W. & A. G. C. Grandison. 1977. *Snakes— A Natural History*. British Museum (Natural History), London.

Peters, J. A. & B. Orejas-Miranda. 1970. "Catalogue of the Neotropical Squamata; Part 1, Snakes," *Bull. U.S. Natl. Mus.*, 297(1): 1-347.

Pope, C. H. 1961. *Giant Snakes*. Knopf, New York.

Reichenbach-Klinke, H. & E. Elkan. 1965. *Diseases of Reptiles*. T.F.H. Publ., Neptune, NJ.

Reitinger, F. & J. K. S. Lee. 1978. *Common Snakes of Southeast Asia and Hong Kong*. Heinemann Educational, London.

Ross, R. A. 1978. *The Python Breeding Manual*. Inst. for Herpetological Research, California.

Ross, R. & R. Larman. 1977. "Captive breeding in two species of python, *Liasis albertisii* and *L. mackloti*," *Int. Zoo Yearbook*, 17: 133-136.

Schmidt, K. P. & R. F. Inger. 1957. *Living Reptiles of the World*. Doubleday & Co., Garden City, NY.

Schwartz, A. & R. Thomas. 1975. *A Checklist of West Indian Amphibians and Reptiles*. Carnegie Mus. Nat. Hist., Pittsburgh, PA.

Sheplan, B. R. & A. Schwartz. 1978. "Hispaniolan boas of the genus *Epicrates* and their Antillean relationships," *Annals Carnegie Mus.*, Pittsburgh, PA.

Smith, H.A. & E. D. Brodie,Jr. 1982. *Reptiles of North*

America. Western Publ., Racine, Wisc.

Smith, L. A. 1981. "A revision of the genera *Aspidites* and *Python* (Serpentes: Boidae) in Western Australia," *Rec. West. Aust. Mus.*, 9(2): 211-226.

Smith, M. A. 1943. *The Fauna of British India, Ceylon and Burma. Reptilia and Amphibia. 3. Serpentes.* Taylor & Francis, London.

Stafford, P. J. 1981. "Observations on the captive breeding of Cook's tree boa *(Corallus enydris cookii),*" *Herptile*, 6(4): 15-17.

Stimson, A. F. 1969. "Liste der rezenten Amphibien und Reptilien: Boidae," *Das Tierreich*, 89: 1-49. Walter de Gruyter, Berlin.

Stull, O. G. 1935. "A checklist of the family Boidae," *Proc. Boston Soc. Nat. Hist.*, 40: 387-408.

Todd, S. A. 1976. "Captive breeding of the Indian python *(Python molurus bivittatus),*" *British Herp. Soc. Newsletter*, 14: 25-26.

Tweedie, M. W. F. 1961. *The Snakes of Malaysia.* Govt. Printing Off., Singapore.

Underwood, G. 1976. "A systematic analysis of boid snakes," *In: Morphology and Biology of Reptiles,* Linnean Soc. Symp. 3: 151-175. Academic Press, London.

Wells, R. W. & C. Ross Wellington. 1983. "A synopsis of the class Reptilia in Australia," *Aust. J. Herpet.*, 1(3/4): 105-106.

Worrell, E. 1951. "Classification of Australian Boidae," *Proc. R. Zool. Soc. N.S.W.*, 1949-1950: 20-25.

Wright, A. H. & A. A. Wright. 1957. *Handbook of Snakes of the United States and Canada.* Cornell Univ. Press, NY.

INDEX

Valid species are cross-referenced by specific and generic names. Common names and subspecific names, as well as major synonyms, are referenced to the current generic and specific names. Illustrations are indicated by **bold** page numbers.

Common anaconda: see *Eunectes murinus*
conicus, Eryx; **23,** 108, **112, 138,** 171
constrictor, Boa; **1, 24, 29, 75,** 76, **77, 78, 79,** 82, **126,** 164, 182
constrictor: see *Boa constrictor*
continentalis, Ungaliophis; 116, 180
cookii, see *Corallus enydris*
Cook's tree boa: see *Corallus enydris*
Corallus annulatus; 88, 165
Corallus caninus; 21, **69,** 84, **85, 86, 136, 146,** 165
Corallus enydris; **31,** 84, **87,** 88, 166
crassus, see *Epicrates cenchria*
cropanii, Xenoboa; 159, 170
Cuban boa: see *Epicrates angulifer*
curtus, Python; **16,** 50, 54, **54, 55,** 175
curtus, see *Tropidophis canus*
D'Albert's python: see *Liasis albertisii*
deschauenseei, Eunectes; 168
Diamond python: see *Python spilotes*
dumerili, Acrantophis; 100, **101,** 164, 182
Dumeril's boa: see *Acrantophis dumerili*
dunni, see *Liasis mackloti*
dussumieri, Casarea; 38, 118, **169,** 170, 182
dysodes, see *Tropidophis melanurus*
elegans, Eryx; 171
Emerald tree boa: see *Corallus caninus*
enydris, Corallus; **31,** 84, **87,** 88, 166
Enygrus: see *Candoia*
Epicrates angulifer; 92, **95, 163,** 166
Epicrates cenchria; **7, 27, 35,** 88, **89, 90, 91,** 92, **93, 149,** 166
Epicrates chrysogaster; 167
Epicrates exsul; 167
Epicrates fordii; 92, 94, **96,** 167
Epicrates gracilis; 94, 167
Epicrates inornatus; 94, **96, 162,** 167, 182
Epicrates monensis; 167
Epicrates striatus; **11, 27,** 94, **95, 97,** 167-168
Epicrates subflavus; 94, 168, **169**
ericksoni, see *Tropidophis melanurus*
Eryx colubrinus; **109,** 171
Eryx conicus; **23,** 108, **112, 138,** 171
Eryx elegans; 171
Eryx jaculus; **107,** 108, 171, 182
Eryx jayakari; 110, 171
Eryx johnii; 108, **109,** 110, **111,** 171
Eryx miliaris; 172
Eryx muelleri; 110, 172
Eryx somalicus; 172
Eryx tataricus; **107,** 172

Eunectes barbouri; 168
Eunectes deschauenseei; 168
Eunectes murinus; **5, 13,** 82, **83, 136, 140,** 168
Eunectes notaeus; 82, **83, 85,** 168
European sand boa: see *Eryx jaculus*
exagistus, see *Epicrates striatus*
Exiliboa placata; 116, 118, 159, 178
exsul, Epicrates, 167
familiaris, see *Eryx jaculus*
feicki, Tropidophis; 178
Fischer's boa: see *Epicrates striatus*
fordii, Epicrates; 92, 94, **96,** 167
Ford's boa: see *Epicrates fordii*
fosteri, see *Epicrates striatus*
fowleri, see *Epicrates striatus*
fuscus, see *Liasis mackloti*
gaigei, see *Epicrates cenchria*
galacelidus, see *Tropidophis nigriventris*
Garden tree boa: see *Corallus enydris*
gigas, see *Eunectes murinus*
Gongylophis: see *Eryx conicus*
gracia, see *Lichanura trivirgata*
gracilis, Epicrates; 94, 167
granti, see *Epicrates monensis*
Green anaconda: see *Eunectes murinus*
Green tree boa: see *Corallus caninus*
Green tree python: see *Chondropython viridis*
greenwayi, Tropidophis; **115,** 179
gularis, Trachyboa; 115, 116, 178
haetianus, Tropidophis; **117,** 179
hapalus, see *Epicrates gracilis*
hardyi, see *Tropidophis nigriventris*
hemerus, see *Tropidophis haetianus*
hygrophilus, see *Epicrates cenchria*
imbricatus, see *Python spilotes*
imperator, see *Boa constrictor*
Imperial python: see *Python molurus*
inornatus, Epicrates; 94, **96, 162,** 167, 182
jaculus, Eryx; **107,** 108, 171, 182
Jamaican boa: see *Epicrates subflavus*
jamaicensis, see *Tropidophis haetianus*
Javelin sand boa: see *Eryx jaculus*
jayakari, Eryx; 110, 171
Jayakar's sand boa: see *Eryx jayakari*
johnii, Eryx; 108, **109,** 110, **111,** 171
Keel-scaled boa: see *Casarea dussumieri*
Kenyan sand boa: see *Eryx colubrinus*
kinghorni, see *Python amethistinus*
lanthanus, see *Tropidophis greenwayi*
Liasis albertisii; 62, **63,** 173